"Everyone has a story and Debbie Eckert has given us the joy of sharing hers in this insightful book. This is more than a memoir; it is a beautiful testimony of love. Her folksy, down-home way of writing is charming. It is not necessary for you to have exactly the same philosophy, theology, or spirituality that Debbie has, for this book to bless you. You will be drawn in by her passionate relationship with Jesus. Her faith just might make you sit down and pray for a multiplication of faith in your own life."

Macrina Wiederkehr, O.S.B., retreat guide, and author of *Abide: Keeping Vigil with the Word of God and Seven Sacred Pauses*

"Nothing about Debbie Eckert is boring or dull - lucky for those who know her, or those who know her only by this exciting book. Her years of growth in faith have led her to be able now to speak fearlessly and with ruthless honesty about the ups and downs of her own spiritual journey, and by sharing her life to give others the courage to seek their true destiny in God."

Former Abbott of Subiaco Monastery **Jerome Kodell O.S.B.,** whose books include: *Don't Trust the Abbott: Musings from the Monastery, Twelve Keys to Prayer*

HAIRSPRAY, HOLY WATER & THE HEALING HAND OF GOD

Debbie Eckert

ISBN-13: 978-1-7330625-0-3

Typeset by Amnet Systems

TABLE OF CONTENTS

FORWARD

by
Fr. John Marconi

I have known Debbie Eckert for most of my 31 years in the Priesthood. Our paths have crossed in both the Cursillo Ministry and Charismatic Movement in the Diocese of Little Rock. From the very moment I met her, she and her family became part of my family. I lovingly call her "Sis," because in every sense of the word she is that to me. She is my sister in Christ.

I have spent much time at the Eckert home and have been blessed to witness the Eckert family through all their ups and downs and through their joy and pain. Even some of my nieces and nephews call her Aunt Debbie as they have heard me call her "sis" many times. I say this to let you know the depth of my relationship with her and how much she and her family mean to me.

Over the years, I have been the beneficiary of many haircuts at Debbie's Hair and Prayer, her salon. Every compliment I get about my hair goes to Debbie, my hairdresser, and, oh, so much more. As you read this book, you too will discover what she has to offer when you sit in her chair. I have prayed for her and her family as if they were my own and I have been the beneficiary of her prayers for all these years.

I am very familiar with most of the stories and witnessing you will read in this book and have even been a part of some of them. I am very grateful to God that they are now written for you to read and that what I have known for many years about how God has worked through my Sis Debbie others will soon know. We have grown together spiritually on this faith journey and are currently blessed to be working together as Spiritual Directors for our Diocese.

Our faith journey even saw me as her Pastor at St. Joseph's in Conway, from 2010 to 2016. During those six years, I had to walk a delicate balance of loving her and Kenny but also making it very clear that at that time I was their Pastor/Shepherd.

She still cut my hair at Debbie's Hair and Prayer, and I did my best to maintain a shepherd's heart toward my people, so I was reluctant many times to say much, while in the ministry chair at Debbie's. We all know how things are talked about at the hairdresser's. Many people tried to cross the line at times, but we both knew it, and all went well.

However, as her Pastor/Brother for those years, I could not have been more proud of my Sister/Sheep. One day she approached me and wanted to begin an intercessory prayer time before our 10:30 a.m. Mass. I immediately said yes, and encouraged many people to go to her and the other intercessors for prayer. What a blessed ministry they provide for God's people. If only in all our parishes there would be others to stand up and be intercessors. What a difference that would make to so many of our brothers and sisters in the body of Christ. This demonstrates the heart of prayer that Debbie has, and continues to have. Even to this day, when I need intercessory prayer, she is my first contact on the battle line.

In *Holy Water and Hairspray*, you are going to read many stories of how God works in lives for those who believe and trust in Him. As she shares her stories, she would like you to know as well that God is a Great God, and is always near to answer the prayers of His Children. I recommend a slow reading at the end of each chapter to reflect upon your own faith journey.

For those who are lost, you can find greater purpose and meaning in your life. For parents who struggle at times raising children, see how prayer can carry you and sustain you in dark times. For those in ministry, you can find the courage to step out in faith. For those looking for deeper walk with God, listen to what God has for you in these pages.

For those who know that God is calling them to be a "shofar," don't be afraid of allowing God to use you as His messenger of Hope in these trying times. In this book the Shofar (Debbie), is proclaiming the Good News, to wake us up in faith and know that God is with us and victory is near.

> *Let nothing upset you,*
> *let nothing startle you.*
> *All things pass;*
> *God does not change.*
> *Patience wins*
> *all it seeks.*
> *Whoever has God*
> *lacks nothing:*
> *God alone is enough*
>
> *- St. Teresa Avila*

INTRODUCTION

I want to begin with a short story to introduce you to this book. Many years ago, I was trying to discern whether to stay or leave my position as the Executive Director for the Cursillo movement in Arkansas. Cursillo is a program that aims to help people come into a personal relationship with God. My faith was growing at this time and I didn't want to miss God's voice or direction. I might also add that my faith was still a bit immature, but I was truly trying to follow God's lead. I was on my way to a Secretariat meeting for this ministry when I asked God for a sign to help me discern my decision. Some people refer to this as laying a fleece when trying to make a decision. This practice comes from Judges 6 when Gideon asked God for a sign. He wanted to know if it was God speaking to him.

I had about a thirty-minute drive to the meeting and for some reason, and I don't know why, I asked God to let me see a deer if I was to stay. Deer weren't really a special love of mine at that time, but that's the fleece I laid out. When I got to the meeting, I told our Spiritual Director what I had done. To this day I can remember what he said to me. He said: "Debbie that's kind of dangerous, but we will pray about it." I sure didn't see a deer on the way there, and I was beginning to think I was about to leave this ministry. On my way home, several hours later, I was praying and talking to God about this position when I looked up and saw seven deer in a field by the interstate. I couldn't believe my eyes. God had truly spoken to me. I was amazed, and so my communing with God through the deer began.

The sign of the deer began to be a regular occurrence for me when trying to make a decision. Never in my life had I seen deer like this and now I was seeing them all the time. Each time I would see them I would think of the verse from **Psalm 42:1 NRSV As a deer longs for flowing streams, so my soul longs for you, O God.** I was seeing deer so much that I began to ask God if my love for Him was not enough. When I would see them, I would say to God: "I love you Lord. Help me love you more each day." I would see them in some of the most peculiar places.

After several years of this, I was on my way to my office at the Catholic Diocese of Little Rock because I was still in the position for the Cursillo ministry as well as being a hairdresser with my own salon. During the drive, I saw several deer. I said: "OK, Lord, I know I started this, but what are you trying to tell me? You sure have shown me a lot of deer over the years." I told the Lord that I loved Him very much and then what happened next took me a bit by surprise. Not in audible voice, but an interior one, I clearly heard God say: "All I'm trying to tell you is that I "deerly" love you!" I teared up as I realized what I had just heard.

Finally I had a sense of why I was allowed to see so many deer for all those years. God was trying to breakthrough to me. He speaks to each of us, if we but take the time to listen. I had not realized, or put it all together until years later at a silent retreat, that God was also represented as a stag in the scriptures. Not only was He saying that He "deerly" loved me but that His presence was always with me and within me. To this day, God still speaks to me through the deer. Just to make sure I believed what I had heard interiorly, God spoke again in an absolute way.

Now it was a regular occurrence that our then Bishop Andrew J. McDonald would send me an inner office memo to bring my clippers and scissors so I could cut his hair. He was a beautiful spirited man, God rest his soul. I was still smiling from the word the Lord had given me when I entered the conference room to cut his hair. I told him the story about how the deer had become such an important voice and sign of God for me. I then told Bishop Andrew that Psalm 42:1 would always come to my mind and I would question God why I was seeing them so frequently. I did not tell Bishop Andrew what I had just heard God say to me on the drive to the diocese. As I shared the story of the deer with him he listened intently. When I finished talking, he looked up at me with his gentle eyes and said: "Perhaps God is just telling you that He "deerly" loves you." I couldn't believe what I had just heard. God used this very holy man to confirm what I had heard interiorly and to help me to have an understanding of the love God had for me.

He wants us all to know how much He loves us. God was also training me to hear His voice. He wants you to come to know His voice as well. We hear in *John 10:27: My sheep hear my voice, and I know them, and they follow me.* Many people, especially my friends, came to know about the "deer." So much so, that a few of them asked to see a deer or I would ask on their behalf and they would see them as well.

God wants you to know that He "deerly" loves you!

It is my desire that as you read through these pages your love for our Lord will grow and that you will become keenly aware that God is always with you. He wants to speak to you uniquely just as He does to me and so many others. Even as I share this story, God is allowing me to go deeper into this experience. That's what happens when God gives us these personal experiences. We savor them and can keep going deeper into the graces.

Why Hairspray, Holy Water and The Healing Hand Of God?

As you read through the pages of this book, it is my desire that you do not see me but our mighty God who has been so generous to me and those that I love so dearly. This is really a story about our awesome God. My one desire for the outcome of this book would be that you would see the heavens open and that the glory of God would fall upon you as you grow closer to our Father while reading the pages of this book. As you grow closer to Him, linger with him in conversation. Lap up the water from His refreshing streams. Meander along the pages of this book and rest in the verdant spots that He gives you repose. These are places that the Holy Spirit wants you to be present with Him. Maybe it will be a place of challenge, or a sweet memory of your own experience of His love for you. Ask Him questions and then <u>listen</u> for the answer.

As you read earlier, I am a hairdresser. I have spent forty-six years of my life standing behind a chair and most of my life has been spent in service to others. Hair spray has been a mainstay in my career as a hairdresser and it's actually very symbolic to me as I ponder my relationship with the Lord.

Here are just a few examples of how God is like hairspray: he keeps us in the right place if we let him, he holds us up when we are weak, He forms us into his image and He gives us lasting power to go the distance. It is common for people to say: "Give me a good shot of hairspray; I'm going to need it with the day ahead of me." So it is with God, we need him to be with us and give us that ability to hold up.

Each day, for all of the years I've been a hairdresser, I have also heard the same things repeated over and over.

"My hair is dirty, I need it washed today."

"I need a complete change, I feel so drab and dull."

"I need some color put on to brighten me up and add a little zest."

And then there's the "Don't change my hair, I'm comfortable like this." Or "I feel like a new person!" "I really needed a change today." "Thank you for listening to me today."

I never realized how much of what I do is like what happens to us as we are immersed into the Holy Water when we are baptized. Original sin requires a need for cleansing. We need the baptismal waters to purge those things in us that need change. We are given a newness of life. Some days the changes are subtle and other days they are dramatic. Adding the Holy Spirit in this whole process adds the color and zest to our lives. We leave the baptismal waters a new person and we are the better for it. It is those who don't want change, who are comfortable to stay like they are that have a harder time adjusting to the places that the Lord might lead them on this journey we call life. God will meet us in our everyday natural places, which in my case is the beauty salon and my home. He will transform our natural environments into the supernatural. It's a hairspray and Holy Water transformation all while we are holding that healing hand of God.

Some days the flow of our life will be effortless and other days it will seem like the stream of life has dried up. It is there that God wants to reveal himself to us: in the ordinary everyday events. Just as he changed the water into wine, taking something very ordinary and changing it into something very extraordinary, so He desires to touch the very minutes of the days of our lives and transform them into extraordinary time spent with Him. I have come to know that in suffering holiness is produced. It is in those times that we grow the most. At first the suffering may look like hair color gone bad, but with the professional (Jesus) at the other end of the color bottle, our bad hair days are turned into beautiful creations that reflect the character of Jesus.

The pages of this book are filled with story after story of God's mercy, all the while loving, healing, and wooing myself and others to His tender heart and then holding us with his healing hands. He is always reaching out to us. I believe that it is possible for all Christians to witness miracles, signs and wonders in our everyday life. This is normal Christianity, but it takes an active participation with the Holy Spirit. The Holy Spirit is the power in each of us that is given by God to do those greater signs than Jesus did while on earth. *"Truly, truly, I say to you, he who believes in me will also do the works that I do; and greater works than these will he do, because I go to the Father. - John 14:12-14*

When we seek the Father's will, tap into the resurrected power of Jesus and co-labor with Him, nothing is impossible! May God color your life beautifully and deeply as He has touched mine! May you know that God "deerly" loves you and that with Him, there's always hope!

CHAPTER 1

FINDING YOUR PURPOSE

W hat is your purpose in life? Do you believe that God has a plan and purpose just for you? A purpose for which you were created? God the Father called you and me forth. He willed that we should be born. He has a plan and a purpose for my life and He has a plan for your life as well. As you read a bit about me and a lot about how God has worked in my life, my desire is that you will see your purpose in the kingdom more clearly and that these pages will stoke up a fire in your heart that will set the world ablaze!

My beginnings were meager but each event in my life had an important part in the way the next day would play out and the day after that and the day after that. *God said let there be life and we are created.*

We come into this world free and naked. As life progresses, we somehow can lose our freedom and cover ourselves with many masks until sometimes it takes a major shift to bring us back to true north. I had some shakings to point me back to my true self and as I reflect back on these I see that they were some of the greatest graces in my life. Some days we are pruned and some days we are fertilized and watered. We are God's tender vine and He is the vinedresser. As you read this chapter, I want to paint you a picture of my childhood so that you can see how my early years affected my spirituality that developed as I matured. These early years gave me the ability to see God in all things, developing in me a deep love for nature and simple things. It is very easy for me to see the grandeur of God in a butterfly or the symphony of crickets and frogs singing on a summer night. As you read this chapter, remember your own early years of formation. Stop and pause along the way to savor the good memories and bring the not-so-good memories to the Lord. So let me start in the beginning where we all must start.

My home life as a child was one of very simple standards. I was number four in the family of five children starting with my oldest brother Theodore, who is 20 years older than me; then my sister Bernadine, who is 18 years older; my sister Brenda, who is eight years older than me; and my younger brother Robert, who is eight years younger than me. As you can see we were very spread apart in age. Since we were so spread out in age, I never lived at home with all of them at the same time, which made for some interesting dynamics in our family. It was common for all of our families to gather often at my parents' home. Somehow, that farm and our parents kept us bonded together. I never knew how deeply my spirit was tied to that land until I moved away. It is a gift to have deep roots, whether it be in family or faith, preferably both.

I grew up in a place that many would call Camelot. Our farm was a place where a kid could discover and imagine. Our farm had all the things one would expect on a farm: cattle, pigs, horses, chickens and tractors. The farm was a place I was safe, except for the occasional snakes and other crawling things. I knew that I was loved and well cared for. My summer days were spent hoeing weeds in the garden, fishing, watching the flowers bloom, and chasing fireflies as they lit up the night sky. The sweet sounds of the whip-poorwill and hooting of the owl was like a symphony that I tuned into each night. These are mystical gifts of nature that one should pay attention to for they show us the creative nature of our awe-some God!

We had ponds, creeks, frogs, and barns. I had my own fairy-land as I entertained myself on that beautiful farm. Our family farm was a place where my spirituality was nourished at an early age. I could see God's hand all around me in His creation. It was where I could daydream of faraway places, compose songs in my heart, get my feet and hands dirty, and become one with the earth. Our land was a place that taught me how to be alone with myself and to do a lot of quiet meditation. Our farm was my first school. It taught me much about having a contemplative spirit. There were times that I was lonely, but this taught me to be more present with God. As a young child, I talked to Him a lot.

We didn't have junk food so I knew where to find the wild fruits such as blackberries, muscadines, and persimmons. These were my treats. There was the rhythm of seasons in the natural world, just like we have in our own life and our spiritual life. Persimmons ripened in the fall so if you tried to eat a persimmon before it was ripe, you got a taste of bitterness that you would not soon forget. Blackberries were too tart if picked green and musca-dines were not juicy or sweet if plucked too soon. As a child I was being taught lessons that I would apply in my life as I grew older. I was being taught that some things cannot be hurried. You can-not force fruit to ripen before its time and expect the best results. These lessons apply to more than fruit; often we pray for things that don't arrive when we want them. But, God's timing is perfect, as I will show in the upcoming chapters. I also learned that there are some things you just don't eat. For example, some mushrooms are poisonous. I would later learn in life, that you cannot have a diet of unhealthy life choices without serious consequences. What we take into our minds and bodies will eventually come out either for good or for bad.

⇥⇤

WE FISHED A LOT IN THE EVENINGS on our ponds. I loved being able to spend time with my daddy fishing. He taught me many things while fishing: how to bait a hook, what type of bait to use, how to set the hook when the fish nibbles, where fish are likely to be so you have a better chance to catch one, which fish likes a particular habitat, and how to be patient. I also came to know that some days the fish just don't bite! It was exciting to think that I might catch a big fish, but I was always happy to catch any size. The days fishing with my dad are still teaching me.

Do you see where this is going? I see so many comparisons, when I think of those days and apply them to things of God. When I am working in the kingdom, I have to know what type of bait to use to catch a fish. What do I say? Where are the fish? Help me to have patience Lord and to realize that catching the fish is dependent on you and your grace. Where do you want me to fish? What fish do you want me to catch? You see, Jesus calls us to fish for souls! Sometimes you get nibbles, sometimes you don't even get a bite, but sometimes, you catch a really big fish. Of course, all souls in God's eyes are big fish. What is the value of one soul?

> *As he walked by the Sea of Galilee, he saw two brothers,*
> *Simon who is called Peter and Andrew his brother,*
> *casting a net into the sea; for they were fishermen. And*
> *he said to them, "Follow me, and I will make you fishers*
> *of men."*

> **—Matthew 4:18-19**

The garden had its own lessons to teach. Our garden was huge. It provided much of the food we consumed through the year. We didn't have an irrigation system for our garden so we depended upon the rain to come at the appropriate times. This sure does help a person keep their eyes heavenward asking the good Lord for a bountiful yield in the garden. Too much rain on some vegetables was a disaster and not enough rain also presented its own set of problems. All good gardeners know that you have to keep the weeds out of the garden to keep them from choking out the vegetables. My momma and daddy prided themselves on having a pretty garden, so my summer days regularly included pulling or hoeing weeds. I didn't mind doing this for the most part. However, I did experience some fear and trepidation because you never knew when you might find that occasional snake coiled up under a tomato plant or under the corn stalks. Once in a while, you might even find one hanging from the stalks when you reached in to pick something. In addition to removing the choking weeds, we also learned to apply proper fertilizer to increase the yield.

Applying the lessons from the garden to my faith life, I see so many similar analogies. Let's compare the garden to our souls. If we are to produce much fruit for the kingdom, the garden of our soul must have proper nourishment. We must have daily prayer time and proper nutrients in our time with God. Daily scripture reading, contemplative prayer, meditation, contrition, thanksgiving, and adoration all keep the soul properly nourished. I know that if I'm praying through the day with this attitude, I'm more likely to have a great day. However, my life experience tells me that I'm sure to meet up with the noon-day devils along the way. He's hidden and coiled up like the snakes in the garden. The snake's coloring is so compatible with the environment that you have to be aware of your surroundings and be on guard! I don't want to bring attention to this tormentor, but he is real.

Be sober, be watchful. Your adversary the devil prowls around like a roaring lion, seeking someone to devour.

—1 Peter 5:8.

Much of our battle with the enemy is being prepared and on guard, just like I learned to do as a child when in the garden. Keep the armor on!

Finally, be strong in the Lord and in the strength of his might. Put on the whole armor of God, that you may be able to stand against the wiles of the devil. For we are not contending against flesh and blood, but against the principalities, against the powers, against the world rulers of this present darkness, against the spiritual hosts of wickedness in the heavenly places. Therefore take the whole armor of God, that you may be able to withstand in the evil day, and having done all, to stand. Stand therefore, having girded your loins with truth, and having put on the breastplate of righteousness, and having shod your feet with the equipment of the gospel of peace; besides all these, taking the shield of faith, with which you can quench all the flaming darts of the evil one. And take the helmet of salvation, and the sword of the Spirit, which is the word of God. Pray at all times in the Spirit, with all prayer and supplication. To that end keep alert with all perseverance, making supplication for all the saints,

—Ephesians 6:10-18

As I mentioned before, we had cattle on our farm. I always had a few favorite cows. As you spend time with them, you learn they have personalities just like humans. The cows had daily habits they followed. They would always come up in the evening to graze in the field near our house. I'm not sure why this was their habit because I don't remember daddy feeding them there, but this was what they did each day. One of the things that the Lord is reminding me about is how they stayed together in the herd. If there was a storm, the whole herd headed to the barn or a place of natural shelter. If they grazed, they all grazed together. They had an intuitive awareness to know to stay together as a group. If there was ever a cow alone, separated from the herd, my daddy knew to go check on it. It could be calving, or sick or caught in a dangerous situation. If the cows have the sense to stay together in common groupings, shouldn't we? I know from my own personal experience that as a Christian, I must stay connected with other Christians. This happens when I worship communally or when I participate in Bible studies with a group, or even when I spend time in spiritual direction with my spiritual director. We need the direction of a faith community. We need communal worship.

And let us consider how to stir up one another to love and good works, not neglecting to meet together, as is the habit of some, but encouraging one another, and all the more as you see the Day drawing near.

—Hebrews 10: 24-25

The cows were blessed to have my daddy as the herdsman. He knew his cattle, and the cattle knew him. He had his own personal way of calling them, and they responded because they trusted him. This trust was built over time. He kept a close watch on them. He gave them medicine when they were sick, and he knew if one was missing. He knew just how to handle a cow that strayed off from the herd. We have that kind of loving herdsman. Our Papa in heaven watches over us with such tender care. He knows everything that is going on with us. He gently guides us to the places to graze, he binds up our wounds, and he is merciful when we stray. Do you know the voice of your Papa who is your herdsman? Do you know the voice of your shepherd?

I am the good shepherd; I know my own and my own know me

—John 10:14

I was taught the value of hard work. My brothers and sisters and I were expected to do things around the house to help that were age appropriate. I helped in the kitchen, the garden, and did light housework such as dusting and hanging clothes on the line. As I got older, I helped with the wood chores because we had a wood burning stove in our house. I tossed a bale or two of hay, and with the large garden, there were always vegetables or fruits that needed picking or cleaning. As I look back, I know that the work ethic that was instilled in me as a child growing up is what has helped me to have a strong work ethic as an adult. I am very appreciative of my home training now. These daily chores made me know that if you want something bad enough, you have to work for it. We didn't have great financial means, but we always had what we needed. Looking back, I am sure that my mama and daddy had to depend on divine providence. I didn't really know the sacrifices they made daily for us. I had clothes that were made from feed sacks, and I was proud to have them! We raised out own meat and actually slaughtered the animals that we consumed.

It really was such a different world than what most children grow up in today. Looking back, I know why I was told "no" to my requests for dance lessons and scouts and things like that. We just didn't have the money for those things. You didn't buy things unless you had the money for it. If you bought something, there had to be a need, it had to last for a long time, and you didn't throw it away just because it was old or you were tired of it! I still buy clothes today thinking I need to be able to grow into them! Problem is at age 62, I have the middle-age spread and I do grow into my clothes! We never threw away food. Leftovers were always used in some way.

> *And when they had eaten their fill, he told his disciples, "Gather up the fragments left over, that nothing may be lost." So they gathered them up and filled twelve baskets with fragments from the five barley loaves, left by those who had eaten.*

> **—John 6:12-13**

Jesus used everything! I know there is a deeper spiritual teaching here, but He used a meal to show us how to use everything and not waste.

WALKING HOME from where the bus dropped me off was quite an adventure for a seven-year-old girl. I went to Catholic schools but the public bus system picked us up at our school every day. The problem was that we lived in another school district so the bus dropped me off almost a mile and a half from my house. This meant that I had to walk down a dirt road that was overgrown and pretty scary when you're alone. You would never do that now, but things were very different then. Some days my imagination would run wild and I would be so scared that I would stop at the first house on the road and call my married sister to see if she had the car that day to come and pick me up. I had all kind of excuses of why she needed to come and get me. I don't really ever remember telling the actual truth that I was just plain scared. I composed many songs, and stopped for an occasional blackberry or to pick a wild rose along the way. That long walk each day taught me to have courage. I had an imaginary sword that I planned to use when I crossed the swayed overgrown bridges. A monster just might jump out and I would have to defend myself!

There are some times in life that you just have to go it alone – or so we think. What I am saying is that while we have Christian community and friends, sometimes all they can do is just support us; they can't really carry the burden or walk the walk for us. Those times when we are called to walk that lone mile, our Lord is always with us.

> *Teaching them to observe all that I have commanded you; and lo, I am with you always, to the close of the age.* **Matthew 28:20** and again in **Revelation 21:3**
> *And I heard a loud voice from the throne saying, "Behold, the dwelling of God is with men. He will dwell with them, and they shall be his people, and God himself will be with them;*

My mother taught me to sew. This gave me the blessing of learning how to create something that was useful but also pretty. I get a feeling of accomplishment when I'm in a creative mode. It is pretty awesome to take some material, have the vision to see what the potential is, and then begin to create your vision. My mother had that knack. She could go into the yard, the meadow or the woods, gather a variety of plants and flowers, and end up with a pretty arrangement. Cooking is like that as well. You start out with a variety of different ingredients and end up with something tasty. Very seldom did I see her use a recipe.

My mama would feed you if you were at our house anywhere near mealtime. I think feeding people was how she showed love. It was a gift that she offered anyone who came to our home. One story proves my point about her cooking and hospitality. When my husband Kenny and I were engaged, Kenny was living with several other guys. He was only twenty at this time. His diet consisted mostly of TV dinners, pot pies, and junk food. About ten weeks before we married, he moved into my parent's house to save money and to abandon the roommates he had at the time.

If there was one thing we had in abundance, it was good food. My mama made homemade pasta and sauce and that was a sight to see. If we had steak, she would ask you how many steaks you wanted. Considering Kenny hadn't eaten well in about a year, he ate and ate and ate. When he moved in with us, he weighed 165 pounds; ten weeks later he weighed 210! So now you know what kind of cook she was. I watched my mama and she taught me. There was value in the teaching but more importantly in the time we spent together.

You might be thinking what is the value of this example? I believe that faith is a lot like cooking and sewing. You have to have a vision and then the faith and prayer life to see it come to pass. A person who has a creative imagination has an easier time envisioning God and things of God. I believe it is easier to pray with expectant faith because you have that ability to see beyond what is before you.

> **Now faith is the assurance of things hoped for, the conviction of things not seen.**

> **—Hebrews 11:1**

When that creative part of you is developed, so is your potential to create beautiful things that others can enjoy such as paintings, sculptures, cathedrals, music, and books. The list could go on and on. Michelangelo had that potential; he didn't see a big stone, he saw the potential of what that stone could become: a beautiful carving of the Pieta. God is our first example of the power of creativity. Look at a sunset or sunrise. Are there two that are ever the same? The brilliant hues come and go, all in one glorious event. When I think of the variety of animals and plant life my mind is on overload. If we take the time to look with the eyes of our heart, we can truly capture the grandeur of God's creation as well as the grandeur of God! He is in all. His thumbprint is in all things.

Now that you have been on this journey with me through my early childhood, I want you to take the time to stop once again and think back on your own early years. It is my desire to help you take time to look back, remember, and, maybe, journal some ideas as you take them to the Lord in prayer. Are you thinking the past is in the past, why go there? Yes, it is past, but there is great value on remembering and learning from our past. Do we need to get stuck there? No, but the past travels with us. The experiences of our childhood influence who we are as adults. Many times we bury the good and the not-so-good memories and, in the process, cause problems in the way we see God and others. As good as my childhood was, I have had to deal with many issues that affected me as I grew without me being aware of their impact.

I realize that for some of you reading this, your childhood was far from being anything closely related to Camelot. My story might even stir up some places of jealousy, anxiety or pain that you buried many years ago. Your parents could have been workaholics, abusive to you, or inattentive. Maybe they provided for you materially, but were super-critical and over-demanding. If this is your experience, Jesus wants to heal your past and help you to see that even in the midst of such pain, He can bring good out of every bad circumstance. Jesus wants you to begin to hear the truth and stop believing the lies from hell that the evil one wants to keep you believing. I know as good of parents as I had, they made mistakes that I've had to work on, and I've had to ask for forgiveness from my own four children for mistakes that my husband and I made while parenting them. Our four kids mean the world to us and we didn't intend to do anything but the best for them. However, I know that our best still included some mistakes and for that we are truly sorry. I believe most parents feel this way.

We tend to parent from our experience as we were parented. A wonderful priest once said that you can't be a good father until you have been fathered, and the same is true about being a mom. I would ask those parents who are reading this to stop and take inventory of places that you might need to ask for forgiveness from your own children.

Let's stop right here and take as long as you need to tell Jesus how you feel. Don't hurry through this time with the Lord. If your own children are brought to mind, speak to the Lord about it; if it's about your childhood, then take it to the Lord. As He brings up hurts from the past, just hand them over to Him. Ask Him to touch the deepest part of your being and bring the healing balm of Gilead.

The healing balm of Gilead is Jesus' precious blood shed for you. Also, remember that for healing to happen, we need to come to a place of forgiveness to the one who has hurt us. We do this to free ourselves from the pain and the hurt. This doesn't mean that the hurt was justified. It is saying that you don't want the pain to have power over you anymore. What is brought from the darkness into the light has no more power over us.

Isaiah 49:9 says: **saying to the prisoners, 'Come forth,' to those who are in darkness, 'Appear.' They shall feed along the ways, on all bare heights shall be their pasture;** I John 12:46 *says* : **I have come as light into the world, that whoever believes in me may not remain in darkness.**

Let it go!!

Now that you have been still before the Lord, may I offer a starter prayer?

"Jesus, all my life I have believed that _____ _____ (place your prayer need here). I now praise you for I am fearfully and wonderfully made. Your works are wonderful, I know that full well, but somehow I have come to believe the lies of the enemy camp. Listen to what the psalmists says about you. *I praise thee, for thou art fearful and wonderful. Wonderful are thy works. Thou knowest me right well; Psalm 139:14* Please go back into the places I am wounded and heal me. I also extend forgiveness to those who have hurt me. I know that I cannot do this on my own, so please give me the grace to forgive those who have hurt me. Please do that through me sweet Jesus. Help my mind to be healed from the lies I have believed. *1 Corinthians 2:16 says "For who has known the mind of the Lord so as to instruct him?" But we have the mind of Christ.* Renew my mind from stinking thinking. Help me to believe that I am formed in the image and likeness of you God. Restore my dignity as a child of God. Heal me, renew me, and help me to truly think like you do Lord. I plead your precious blood over myself and my needs and I thank you for the powerful way you are going to heal me. Help me Lord to believe your word in its entirety.

"Dear Father in heaven, I ask that you heal my children from any negative consequences that we as parents might have caused. Please restore the years that the locust have eaten as it says in **Joel 2:25.** *I will restore to you the years which the swarming locust has eaten, the hopper, the destroyer, and the cutter, my great army, which I sent among you.*

We were the locusts at times Lord and for this we are truly sorry. Renew my children with your love and grace. You, Jesus, are the Divine physician and you can heal my children and me by the power of your blood. We ask this in your name sweet Jesus."

Now let me continue with my story.

≕╪╞≔

CHAPTER 2

MY TWO MAMAS

Our family was what you would describe as a strong Catholic family. My parents defined a strong Catholic family as one with a legacy from generations past on both sides, a tradition of Catholic education, and obedience to church laws and traditions. I don't remember ever missing Sunday Mass. My parents sent us to Catholic schools even though I'm sure that was a tremendous sacrifice. We prayed the rosary daily with the extended family that lived in close proximity. My parents didn't read the Bible to me that I can recall. I do know, however, that they lived what the Bible contained. I don't remember discussions about personal relationships with Jesus. I didn't really know what that meant, but I knew I wanted to obey God's laws because I wanted to be a good Catholic.

My Catholic school and community was the other world I grew up in. I was taught by the School Sisters of Notre Dame through my twelve years of schooling. I remember Latin Masses and the Baltimore Catechism. I could rattle all the memorized doctrine like a champ. I loved school because it brought me into a world of knowledge and I was hungry to learn. I admired the sisters and the priests because they represented something good and holy and I wanted to be like them. Priests were plentiful in the early Sixties. The strong presence of professed religious belief influenced my spirituality more than I realized at that time. I can even remember thinking that I wanted to be a sister. I guess all Catholic kids at that time wanted to be a nun or a priest or at least considered it. Perhaps that desire was true in my spirit as I look at my life now. I am serving God now in a way I didn't have the ability to envision then.

As a young school girl, I would go into our church during recess. I loved to be in the church sanctuary. I could smell the candles burning and the colors were vivid. The statues and the sun shining through the stained glass windows were the most beautiful images to me. I could feel God's presence when I walked through the doors, but on a lighter side, it was cool in that great big church. You see, it gets hot in the South, and I grew up in a time when few places were air conditioned. I certainly didn't have it at home or at school. In the church, I found some relief from the heat outside.

I am smiling as I think about this. God doesn't waste anything. He used the heat outside to lure me into the cool sanctuary, then He lured me back into the furnace of His loving heart. I would sit in the pews and I was transported into the heavenly realm. I talked to God and Queen Mary, my heavenly mama. I didn't know this was what a personal relationship with God looked like. I just knew that He was pretty important and I wanted to make sure I told Him what I needed. I always felt so protected there. I might have been young, but that tabernacle which contained my Jesus wooed me day after day. I am blessed to still be able to worship in that same church. It is such a wonderful gift to me to have such a faith history to draw from. The nativity set that is used in our church now is the same one I looked at as a child. This evokes such sacred memories.

I'm sure as you read this, you can recall such a place that you went to feel God's presence. Maybe it was under a sturdy oak, or under the stars at night. Did you have a sacred spot? As in the first chapter, I want you to take time to stop and reflect. We will do this together as you journey through the pages of this book. I hope you will enter into the sacred as you pause for quiet meditation. I invite you to stop here for just a moment, and recall your special place where you felt God. Maybe you weren't aware of God's presence as a child. Where is that place for you now? Go there physically or in your mind's eye and sit with Him for a while. Get still and enjoy His company. As you sit with the Lord, look at Him. What does He look like? Is He smiling? Is He speaking to you? Where is He standing in relation to you? Is He touching you? How does this make you feel?

Try to stay out of your head and enter into your heart or your gut where the feelings are stored. Our minds sometimes get us into trouble. Our gut is where truth is. When pondering these questions, sit quietly and just enjoy His presence. When you feel like you've stayed with the presence of the Lord long enough, speak to Him if you have something to say. You need to spend twice as much time in silence as you do in speaking to Him. If you are doing all the talking, how could you be listening to His response?

I believe God is always speaking, we just haven't taken the time to listen. This is one reason why we make so little progress in our prayer time. I think we get bored listening to ourselves!

Are you wondering how much time is enough? Ask the Holy Spirit to give you that number. For some it may be only five minutes of silence, for others maybe thirty minutes, still others maybe an hour. Whatever it is that you hear the Holy Spirit tell you, stay faithful to that time. Don't quit even a few seconds too soon. If you have to set a timer, do so. Sometimes the power of God's revelation to you doesn't come until those last seconds! Many people say they can't hear God. Could we be speaking too much?

JOURNEYING BACK to my days as a first-grader, I remember being told about Our Lady Of Fatima. Sr. Edward Ann told our class the story. I was so intrigued. I believed every word and I had such a desire to see Mary myself. I thought to myself, someday, maybe I will know Mary in this way. As a six-year-old, I reasoned that I needed to be really holy to see Mary. I thought maybe if I'm really good, she'll appear to me one day. What I didn't know then, but that I am aware of now, is that she desires to mother each and every child of God on the planet. My memories of May Crowning of Mary are sweet to me. Every girl wanted to be that one that was picked to do this. I don't recall crowning Mary as a child, but my time would come.

Please allow me to take you on my journey to Mary. The road has been long and she has faithfully stayed by me even when I didn't stay with her. There were times when we got close and then I would always be the one to pull back. If you are not of the Catholic faith, please be open and know that as Catholics, we do not see Mary as God. We venerate her, but we do not worship her. I will share how I was given the revelation of her importance later on. God alone is worthy for worship; but as you read, I hope that you will be open to pondering her role to the body of Christ.

As I grew older Mary was always somewhere in my thoughts and prayers but somewhere in my teenage years, a shift began to happen. I can see clearly now what contributed to that shift, but at the time I wasn't even aware of the changes. I'm going to be transparent in my writing. It's the only way to share truths, in my opinion.

My role and understanding of Mary my mother, paralleled with my own earthly mother. My mother wasn't a very nurturing person to me. I knew she loved me because she showed that through works, but I didn't receive a lot of hugs or words of affirmation from her. In her defense, I don't really think she knew how to give that to me because I don't think she got a lot of it from her mother. She was only eight when her father died and she was one of fourteen children during the very difficult years of the Great Depression. All she knew at that time was how to survive and those skills were carried into her married life as a mother and wife. I'm sure she didn't receive very much one-on-one with her own mother.

We parent as we were parented. My mother modeled hard work and I sure got that imbedded into my soul. It's not all bad because as I stated earlier, I was taught a good work ethic, but it has taken me almost sixty years to get that part of me tempered into right order. My mother worked all the time. Please don't get a negative image of my mother, she was a wonderful lady; but remember even when you live in Camelot, things can get out of balance and need the touch of God. As a young girl, I didn't feel I was missing relational time with my mom, but as years passed things began to change.

My teenage years were lived in the '60s and '70s. It was a time of unrest and change throughout the country. The goodness of my upbringing was tested, as it is for so many in their teens. My parents were so fearful; in fact they parented from a place of fear instead of a place of trust. My mother was the one who communicated as far as parenting. My dad was consulted I'm sure, but mama was the one who spoke to me most of the time. Hang with me for a bit on all of this. As time passed my mother and I got like oil and water. I felt like she didn't trust me, so I might as well do what I wanted because she didn't believe me when I was telling her the truth. This started a great separation between us. As I drifted from my own mother, I also drifted from Mother Mary. My relationship with my mother could not have been more strained.

Please understand that my mother wasn't the only one I place blame on. I contributed to the chasm that was becoming wider and wider. My prayer life was drifting like a boat at sea without a captain. I began to make poor choices and it became easier and easier to choose wrongly.

The deeper you go in the wrong direction, the easier it is to keep going there. In my opinion, two things contribute to this. One is that you begin to listen to the enemy and rationalize and the other is that the farther you get from the truth, the harder it is to make a U-turn. The enemy begins to say things like: "It's OK to have a drink, you'll be OK; the church's teachings on premarital sex are antiquated, you know your situation is different; your parents are stuck in the past, what do they know?"

I give thanks and praise to God that no matter how I was behaving, I continued to go to church. All those years of Catholic schooling and rosary praying were keeping me connected to God in some small way. If you had asked me if I was a faithful Catholic Christian during those years of straying, I would have belted out a "yes, of course" answer! So I continued on slowly, ever so slowly, losing my moral ground.

In my senior year of high school I was chosen to crown Mary at the May crowning ceremony. I was happy to be chosen. I was finally that girl picked to be honored above others. Actually I was happy probably for some wrong reasons. It was a boost to my ego to be picked; and as I look back, I wasn't living in the most virtuous way and there were much better choices among the great young women in my class. I did however, have a thread of admiration for the Blessed Mother that still was alive in me. The desire to try to do what was holy hadn't completely died within me. As I remember, the faculty chose the senior girl to crown Mary, so it was quite an honor.

The day came for May crowning and I was at the lake with friends boating and having a great time. As I look back, I am ashamed today that I almost didn't go to the May crowning. I was having fun and I just didn't want to leave my friends. The forked tongue furnace boy began to tempt me. I was hearing things like: "You don't need to go crown Mary, it's just a statue, they can pick someone else, who will care? You can make up some kind of story and they will never know the truth." There is a real sadness and remorse in my heart today as I reflect back on that day. I thank God that by His grace I had enough strength to do the right thing that sunny spring day. My mama Mary was desiring me to come closer and I just could not hear her sweet voice clearly. I know now that in coming closer to her, she would keep me closer to her son. Mary always draws us to her son Jesus. This would not be the last time she made her motherly presence known to me.

Eventually I married my husband, Kenny, and I was out from under the roof of my mother. Things became a bit better between us; however, we never seemed to be able to get back to a place of ease in conversation. Her worry and fear always seemed to creep in and my strong will of wanting to be right contributed in a big way. I wish I could say that our relationship eventually got better but it never really did. Just as my Mother Mary wanted a relationship with me, my mama Rose wanted a healthy relationship with me as well. We just couldn't seem to find our way to each other.

It is important to stop now and tell you about the spark of faith that was still in me and how that spark began to ignite. Kenny and I never quit going to Mass each Sunday. One particular Sunday we heard about a program called Renew that our church would be starting. Renew was a small faith-sharing group that met weekly with other church members.

We had been married about 10 years by now and things were getting difficult. We had two of our four children and some struggles were starting to present themselves. The grace of God hit us that Sunday. We looked at each other in church and agreed we would sign up right then and there. It was a wonderful time of growth for us both. We met some great couples and the Holy Spirit really began to work in our lives.

Actually, the Holy Spirit was always there, we just finally started to respond to the Spirit. We began to hear about Charismatic prayer groups, including Cursillo, a movement in the Catholic Church, and I was gently invited to join a Protestant Bible study called Bible Study Fellowship. We began to experience growth in our faith life and in our marriage in a very powerful way.

As you begin to get closer to the Lord, the Holy Spirit begins to gently shine a light on places that need to be confessed and healed. I was being convicted to admit to my mother that I had been horrible at times to her. These feelings churned and churned inside of me. A few years passed, and the beginning stages of Alzheimer's hit my mother and it came with a vengeance, swift and hard. She was only in her late sixties.

I was very angry with God. Just when I was finally ready to work on our relationship as mother and daughter she was slipping away at an unbelievable rate. I remember telling God it was unfair. I had never gotten the mother I wanted. "Why is this happening now, God? I want to have a mama I can talk to without fighting." All I heard in response from God was to quit concentrating on what I didn't get and concentrate on what I did receive from my mother. The Lord was speaking to my heart, but I only heard it with my head.

My mother was slipping away and I did as much as I could for her as she progressed in this terrible illness. It was so hard. I had small children and being around her in this condition was more than I could take.

Looking back, my anger was still brewing inside of me. When someone you love gets ill, no matter what the disease is, I think you begin to also deal with your own mortality. This was happening to me and I was not only angry but scared as well. This was a period of great guilt for me. I just felt like no matter what I did, it wasn't enough.

I know now that the guilt was mostly from the enemy camp. Add the guilt and anger, along with the financial burdens this began to cause our siblings for extended care, and you had a mess. Thankfully I had Bishop Andrew J. McDonald, to whom you were introduced in the introduction. I was very close to him at this time and he helped steer me and my conscience in right order.

As we continue to grow closer to the Lord, we begin to be more obedient to things He asks of us. Our Papa knows us so intimately and He knew how much guilt and pain I was carrying about my mother and our past. He wanted to free both my mother and myself from past hurts while she was still alive.

One day I was giving my mama a perm in her kitchen. She rarely talked at this point and when she did, it didn't make any sense. I heard the Lord interiorly tell me to apologize to her. Even though I wanted to make peace, my pride and strong will resisted. The conversation went on in my head with the Lord something like this:

God: "Tell her you're sorry. . . "
Me: "She won't understand me."
God: "I said to tell her you're sorry for all the things you did that disrespected her. . . remember hitting her with the brush because you didn't want to fix her hair that Saturday morning?. . . Now tell her you're sorry."
Me: "I don't know what good it will do, she doesn't understand a word I'm saying."
God: "Just do as I say.'
Me: "Ok, I will, but it's not going to make things better."

At that moment the grace began to fall as thick as rain in a flood situation. I got eye to eye with my mother and said: "Mama, I'm so sorry for all the times I was disrespectful to you. I'm sorry for hitting you with the brush; I'm sorry for being rebellious." Her eyes made contact with mine. The Lord's presence was palpable and I was aware that my mama was present to me as well. Suddenly, we were in sync with each other and she said to me: "It's OK, I forgive you."

I couldn't believe what I was hearing. We both had been set free. God had given us both so much in just a few minutes. This was the last thing I remember my mother ever saying to me.

She lived 14 years with this horrific disease and even though I was set free in many ways that day in the kitchen, the pain of my desiring more from my mother never completely went away. I had just resolved that it was the way it was and that I couldn't change things. God would continue to heal me as I was open, but that's for later on. I will come back to my mother later. Let me now share a breakthrough that happened with Mary, my queen mother.

Remember when I started this chapter I stated that as a little girl, I wanted to see Mary? Little did I know that I would be given my heart's desire some thirty years later. I didn't actually see Mary, but I experienced her in a fresh new way.

In 1991, I was given the privilege to go to Medjugorje, Yugoslavia. There are many details about this trip that I want to touch on, but one is that my Mother Mary was calling me to renew our relationship. Just like God had called me to get right with my mother, He was wanting me to get right with my heavenly mama.

Since 1981, the alleged apparitions have been taking place in that little hamlet. They still do to this day. The church has not made an official declaration, however, there seems to be a consensus that the early days of the apparitions were authentic. Before I go any farther, my point in this story is how my trip to this place of pilgrimage affected me and those I was with. St. Augustine says in matters of church life (in my paraphrase): In necessary things unity, in undecided things, freedom, and in all things charity. The central message from Mary is prayer, fasting, scripture reading, confession and participation in the sacraments, especially the Eucharist. If you want to know more about these apparitions, here's a place to start. http://www.medjugorje.com/medjugorje.html

Mary was appearing to children in Medjugorje just like she had at Fatima. Many people were experiencing powerful conversions when they traveled there. Mary was calling her children to her Son, Jesus Christ. My father-in-law wanted to send my-mother-in law Verna, my daughter Tara and myself on this trip. Ken, my father-in-law, wasn't Catholic at the time.

My faith was such that I had no problem believing these apparitions were happening; but I didn't have a strong desire to go. Kenny and I had four children by now and our youngest Abbey was only around a year and a half in age. For me to go off and leave my husband to care for this baby and the rest of the household chores was a little beyond my wildest imagination. Kenny was a great husband and father, but areas of domestication were not his expertise.

Without going into great details, circumstances lined up and I was without a doubt sure that we should go. This was a trip I could have never imagined when I was that little girl on the farm. I had barely been out of the state by age 20, let alone to a foreign country, but off we went.

I would be remiss if I didn't tell you that I had the best mother-in-law a person could ever want. I loved Verna probably more than my own mother, especially at this time in my life. My mother had slipped into the pain of her sickness and Verna filled that void that I was so desperately seeking from my own mother.

Not only did we share family, but we shared the Lord as well. We both had a great love for the Lord and a thirst for Him that was unquenchable. Our faith was growing side by side like two vines seeking the sun for nourishment; so it was fitting that we went on this pilgrimage together.

Let me fill you in on a small detail. We should have been afraid to go to this place of pilgrimage, but we weren't. You see, the war had actually started in Yugoslavia at the time. Many groups were not taking pilgrims to the area any longer due to safety reasons, but we were called and off we went.

My first impression of this place was a bit of disappointment. The countryside was beautiful, and it was a quaint little hamlet, but everywhere I looked vendors were selling rosaries and statues and anything else they could market. Where was Mary and where was Jesus?

You see, although I said I believed, there was a part of me that was cautiously testing the spirits. This selling in the marketplace churned inside of me and it was beginning to steal my peace. It bothered me so much that while I was in the confessional with a priest, I told him I was mad about it. He said something to me that I will never forget. He said that Mary was throwing a big party for her son Jesus and many were called to this place to get to know Him. He told me that while I was invited to the party, she wasn't going to be spending as much time with me as the other guests because she knew that I already knew her son pretty well. He told me to be patient and I would get to spend some time with her and that she would help me know her son in an even deeper way. This proved to be true as the week progressed.

The local people were simple, holy people. Even though their country was being torn apart by war, they exuded a peace that permeated the countryside. Many people experience unexplainable phenomena while there, including seeing the sun dance, experiencing a smell of roses in peculiar places, or finding that rosary links turn to gold. The three of us experienced all of these things, but the experience that I must share now is how Jesus manifested His presence to us in the sacraments.

I had a powerful experience that day in the confessional. Mass and praying of the rosary was very powerful as well, but nothing compared to the experience our group had while at the Catholic church in Tihaljina. This was a side trip that we took with our group of about 50 Americans that were mostly youth.

I felt a very strong presence of the Lord when we entered that church. It's very hard to put into words how I felt when we walked through those doors. I felt as if I was on Holy Ground and something very powerful was going to take place. Maybe my experience was something like Moses's experience as He was on Mount Horeb. Should I take my shoes off and prostrate myself before the Lord?

We took our places in the pew and listened to the local priest speak. After he was through speaking, we all lined up in single file next to the communion rail to be prayed over by the priest. As he prayed over each one, the power of the Holy Spirit began to manifest to us. Some were falling or resting in the Spirit, others began to weep, some had demons leave them. This wasn't the first time that I had experienced such things. I was accustomed to the laying on of hands because I was attending a Charismatic prayer group regularly.

After the priest had prayed over each of us, he left and the priest that was with our group as spiritual advisor celebrated Mass in the church. What happened next was the most beautiful experience while on that pilgrimage. This is when Jesus came up to me (at the party that the priest had told me about earlier in the confessional) and said, "Let me show you who I am."

During Mass, at the time that the bread and wine were being consecrated, some of the people began to rest in the spirit. As soon as the priest elevated the host and said: "This is my body" the young people began to fall and rest in the spirit. There were no catchers, they just were going down like bowling pins hitting the terrazzo floors. One young boy was only around seven years old and could never have "faked" it. When Tara, my daughter, received the consecrated host on her tongue, down she went as did some other young people. Bodies were laying everywhere! They were resting in the spirit and Jesus was having His way with them. Jesus IS truly present in the Eucharist.

All that I can give account to here is what my own daughter experienced and what I saw. We finished Mass, prayed the Divine Mercy Chaplet, said a rosary and Tara was still resting in the spirit. I had people help me pick her up and we loaded her on the bus and she didn't awaken until we were down the highway about ten miles later. All in all I would say she rested in the spirit for about 45 minutes. She wept gently and I know that on that day God visited her in a very special way.

Without a doubt I know that Jesus is present, body, soul and divinity in the Eucharist. This was just another affirmation of many along my faith journey about the real presence of Jesus in the Eucharist. Some 27 years later, I asked Tara what she took away from that experience? She said, "Mom, this is the one thing that I know is pure and true. Jesus is real and he is present to us in the Eucharist."

On the way to the church, the bus had been quiet. The tour director tried, but couldn't get the young people to give witness about what they had experienced up to that point on the pilgrimage. On the way back they were fighting over the microphone on the bus. They couldn't wait to share about their experience that day in Tihaljina. Their eyes were opened in the breaking of the bread.

Jesus said: *I am the living bread which came down from heaven; if any one eats of this bread, he will live for ever; and the bread which I shall give for the life of the world is my flesh."*

52 The Jews then disputed among themselves, saying, "How can this man give us his flesh to eat?"

53 So Jesus said to them, "Truly, truly, I say to you, unless you eat the flesh of the Son of man and drink his blood, you have no life in you;

54 he who eats my flesh and drinks my blood has eternal life, and I will raise him up at the last day.

55 For my flesh is food indeed, and my blood is drink indeed.

56 He who eats my flesh and drinks my blood abides in me, and I in him.

57 As the living Father sent me, and I live because of the Father, so he who eats me will live because of me.

58 This is the bread which came down from heaven, not such as the fathers ate and died; he who eats this bread will live for ever." This he said in the synagogue, as he taught at Caper'na-um.

60 Many of his disciples, when they heard it, said, "This is a hard say-ing; who can listen to it?"

61 But Jesus, knowing in himself that his disciples murmured at it, said to them, "Do you take offense at this?

62 Then what if you were to see the Son of man ascending where he was before?

63 It is the spirit that gives life, the flesh is of no avail; the words that I have spoken to you are spirit and life.

64 But there are some of you that do not believe." For Jesus knew from the first who those were that did not believe, and who it was that would betray him.

65 And he said, "This is why I told you that no one can come to me unless it is granted him by the Father."

66 After this many of his disciples drew back and no longer went about with him.

67 Jesus said to the twelve, "Do you also wish to go away?"

68 Simon Peter answered him, "Lord, to whom shall we go? You have the words of eternal life;

69 and we have believed, and have come to know, that you are the Holy One of God." - John 6: 51-69

When we returned home from that trip, my relationship with my Mother Mary was on fresh ground, however I watched my mother go from a beautiful woman who had been strong and giving to a weak invalid.

I so wanted to talk to her, but when I did it was like nobody was home. I would just stare at the physical shell my mother inhabited and pray that she would soon be taken to be with the Lord. She was still able to sit up but rarely spoke. We struggled with care-givers and I watched my dad stand faithfully by her as she leapt into the abyss of that hellacious disease. My mother lived for 14 years after her diagnosis, the last few years in a fetal position. On the day she died, I could smell roses in my bathroom as we were getting ready for church that morning. I should have known that my mother had just left and crossed over to the other side, but It didn't become reality until the call came.

Both of my mothers were reaching out to me through that aroma of roses. For those of you who don't know about the scent of roses, many people smell that fragrance when Mary is present in the room, but since my mother's name was Rose, I believe she was also making her presence known to me one last time.

I wish I could say that my relationship with Mary grew over the years after that trip or that I had finally made peace with losing my mother when I was so young, but life got hectic and I slowly stopped praying the rosary and stopped talking to Mary or asking her to pray for me. I guess I had become enlightened and figured that there was no need to speak to Mary, I could just go straight to Jesus. It is true that we don't have to go through Mary, but I just didn't get the spiritual connection that I could have with Mary until some sixteen years later at a silent retreat.

The pain of not ever having a mother to talk to as an adult woman also got buried on the day of my mama's funeral. I had so many things I wanted to say to my mama. I somehow lost sight of the fact that she was in the communion of saints and was still present to me in a spiritual way just like Mother Mary.

I'll omit the growth that I had experienced up to this point, because I will share that in later chapters. But what I must say as I finish this chapter is that I have now made peace with both of my mothers.

I was attending my third silent retreat when my spiritual director, who was a Catholic priest, gave me some words of wisdom. A silent retreat of eight days has ways of opening up graves where we've buried things from the past if we give God permission to do so. You might be asking why dig up the past? I believe until you deal with old wounds, they will have negative effects on all areas of your life. They must be unearthed and brought into the light of

Jesus and his merciful heart. He wants us to be healed and whole. He took our infirmities upon him.

> *For it is for thy sake that I have borne reproach, that shame has covered my face.*

> **—Psalm 69:7**

> *His face was covered with our shame. But he was wounded for our transgressions, he was bruised for our iniquities; upon him was the chastisement that made us whole, and with his stripes we are healed.*

> **—Isaiah 53:5**

In speaking to my spiritual director, I expressed how I had a difficult relationship with my mother and that I thought that this had come into play with my weak relationship with Mother Mary. I would describe this as a mother wound. He listened to me as I cried and only said one thing to me in response to my conclusion about Mother Mary. He said, "Maybe you are trying to have a relationship with a statue."

He was breaking through to my interior but I still didn't fully get it. Maybe he had said more but all I heard was about the statue relationship and it made sense to me. I began to try to nurture that relationship with Mary once again.

On that retreat, I made some peace with my mama Rose as well. The Lord showed me that she had given me the best she had and had done that in the only way she knew how. I saw her with new eyes and a new heart. Healing had taken place and for that I am grateful. I felt like the healing work was done with my mama Rose. God, however, deals with inner healing in layers. He will do work with you up to the point you can't go much further and then he will let you process the healing and resurface it later until the pain is gone. The scar may still be there; the wound will be healed.

Thinking I was done with my mother wound, another year rolled over on the calendar and it surfaced once again. This time our Lord wanted me to deal with both of my mothers in a particular situation. I was still struggling with the issue although not nearly as bad. I spoke to my spiritual director on my monthly visit and I could feel the tears welling up in me. After the session was over I asked Fr. Mark if I could go into the church and pray for a bit and to listen to God. He opened up the sanctuary for me and I sat in the dark space alone with our Lord.

As I prayed I thought I could feel a drop of liquid falling on my shoulder, but I dismissed it. Another minute or so went by and I felt it again. What was happening? After several more drips I heard these words in my heart. Jesus spoke to me: "I am sorry that you felt unloved. You are precious to Me. I am crying with you over this. . . I am also crying because you have admitted your sinfulness and need for me in your brokenness. These drops are tears of happiness. Some are also tears falling from both of your mothers' eyes. Your mama is sorry for her limitations and failures and Mary is sorry that you felt unloved from your mother for so long. These drops are my tangible presence to you!"

You have to know that I could actually feel wet drops of liquid falling on me. There was moisture on my shoulder. To conclude this tear story, I must tell you that I could have sat in any place in that church but the miracle is that I sat where I did. In a very large church that probably seats over 500 people, I sat where there was a very small leak and I was feeling the slow drips from the rain from the night before. God will use anything to speak to you!

SURELY YOU'RE THINKING how long is it going to take before she finally gets it? This past July, while on yet another eight-day silent retreat, all the pieces finally came together. My spiritual director gave me the verses from **Luke 1: 46-55** to ponder for the next 24-hour period.

46 And Mary said, "My soul magnifies the Lord,
47 and my spirit rejoices in God my Savior
48 for he has regarded the low estate of his handmaiden. For behold, henceforth all generations will call me blessed;
49 for he who is mighty has done great things for me, and holy is his name.
50 And his mercy is on those who fear him from generation to generation.
51 He has shown strength with his arm, he has scattered the proud in the imagination of their hearts,
52 he has put down the mighty from their thrones, and exalted those of low degree;
53 he has filled the hungry with good things, and the rich he has sent empty away.
54 He has helped his servant Israel, in remembrance of his mercy,
55 as he spoke to our fathers, to Abraham and to his posterity for ever."

As I read these verses I began to cry, partly because I could have been Mary saying these verses. I wanted to magnify the Lord, but I also was feeling a stirring about Mary in my heart. As I pondered Mary, thoughts began to surface in my heart and my mind. This is how the prayer and questions began to develop.

"Jesus, you are fully God and fully man. If you are both God and man, you had to have a human egg to become human. That means that you have Mary's DNA in you."

As I prayed over this revelation I began to weep with such remorse on how I had just dismissed Mary so easily. She suddenly became a woman who carried life in the womb, just like me. She nursed Jesus, wiped his snotty nose, cleaned his scrapes and wounds, told stories to him and loved him with all her heart. She was afraid and she was in awe all in the same breath. She loved her son just like I loved my children and she watched him die on the cross. As I pondered how I would feel and how I knew the heart of my children, the sobbing became louder. She was human just like me, only she was the spotless bride of the Holy Spirit. Oh, how I repented and finally I knew. She wasn't a statue, she wasn't just a holy saint in heaven, she was a real woman who God chose.

Now I ask you this: Do you want to tell people about your children? Do you want others to love your children? Do you know what your children love? Do you ask your children to help you with favors for others if it's a good thing? Do you prefer your children to be in the limelight as opposed to you?

If you answer yes to these questions, I ask you why wouldn't Mary want this for her son? She wants us to know her son Jesus. She knows his heart. She knows His desires and she wants to help you love Him as much as she does. Another way to look at this is through your kids' eyes. Do you think your children who love you want others to love you? Do you think that they want others to get to know you? Do you think they might say, let me ask my mom, she can help you because she's good at that. Jesus feels this way about His mama. He wants you to know her. She was chosen to be the mother of our savior.

For those of you who think that as Catholics we worship Mary, this is not true. God alone is worshiped. We do love her and ask her to bring us and our intentions to her son Jesus.

"Oh holy virgin, my mother, come to our aid."

This, my friends, is why we honor Jesus' mother. Jesus honors her and we are to do as He does.

For the rest of my retreat, I not only was aware of my spiritual Mother Mary, I was also aware of my mama Rose in her spiritual state and we walked by the sea together the three of us, hand in hand. We played in the sand, we picked up rocks and shells and we watched the dolphins and the waves and the sunrises and sunsets.

Oh, glorious day! I thank you, Jesus, for the journey to my mothers. I finally see clearly and the three of us will walk together along my earthly journey until you call me home to be with them.

Holy Mary, mother of God, pray for us sinners now and at the hour of our death. Amen

CHAPTER 3
THE WONDER YEARS

I wonder what is going to happen next? I wonder how many children we'll have? I wonder if we will be rich? I wonder if we need to bother going to church? I wonder if you will still love me 50 years from now; and God, why did you let me wander on my own for as long as you did? I wonder if I can wait till tomorrow to start getting serious about you, God? God: Do you wonder how long it's going to take me to get closer to you?

These are questions and thoughts we ask ourselves and God at different times in our life, especially throughout the early years of marriage. In our early years, we have so many questions and we think we have most of the answers. We have a game plan. However, life has its way of putting up detour signs, taking us on a different route to get where we need to go.

Do you remember the board game Life? At times it seems as if we are rolling the dice in the game of life and we have no choices on the outcome of our day-to-day activities. In some cases this can be true; we get surprised. But with God in the mix of daily life, we can make daily choices with discernment and prayer, and then trust His providence with the outcome. Wondering then becomes awe and amazement.

In this chapter I would like to take you into the heart of our marriage: the joys, struggles and victories won with and through God. Hopefully, as we journey in this river of grace, you will do your own reflection and have a clearer picture of how you can journey with God and see His hand being part of all things pertaining to you and your marriage. I am now a 62-year-old wife, mother and grandmother. As I reflect back on the 44 years of my marriage to my soulmate and best friend Kenny, I am in awe of the way God has worked in our lives. I do much less wondering and much more trusting. It would be impossible to cover 44 years in a short chapter, but I want to include some of the highs and lows of those years. Let me say right now that the lows eventually became highs. The lows were opportunities for growth in holiness, so they became treasured gifts. The highs became places of great joy and sacred memories that we could return to when the times were rough.

Keep in mind **Romans 8:28 *We know that in everything God works for good with those who love him, who are called according to his purpose.***

THIS WILL BE a chapter of odds and ends that I think will help you.

I start with our faith life because I believe this is the most important aspect of a marriage. Faith is the glue that keeps things from falling apart, and if something does go awry, your faith life together will mend the brokenness with faith glue. Kenny and I were both cradle Catholics. There was never a time that we didn't attend church together. Somehow, those deep roots from our childhood kept us connected to the body of Christ, even when church attendance for us was more out of the law than desire to honor the Lord.

From day one of our marriage, we said one *Our Father*, one *Hail Mary*, and one *Glory Be* together. We didn't really know how to pray from the heart but we knew we should pray. Meager, yes, but we were at least praying together. We rocked along for about ten years just going through the motions in our faith.

Kenny and I signed up for a program called Renew. It was there that we started to grow as a couple. Our eyes were opened as we read scripture and shared with others in our small group. As I recall one particular Sunday morning, while preparing for our small group, I must share how God's word became fully alive to me the first time in a very personal way. God was trying to get our attention and it was through a financial situation that we were in. Many times it takes some sort of breaking to get us to listen to Him. As long as things are going well we think, who needs God's help?

I sat at my kitchen table that morning with a heavy heart. I couldn't see past the difficult situation we were in. I was worrying and fretting over money and it was consuming me. As I opened the lesson for that morning, God showed up!

I began to read from **Matthew 6: 24-34** *"No one can serve two masters; for either he will hate the one and love the other, or he will be devoted to the one and despise the other. You cannot serve God and mammon.*

25 Therefore I tell you, do not be anxious about your life, what you shall eat or what you shall drink, nor about your body, what you shall put on. Is not life more than food, and the body more than clothing?

26 Look at the birds of the air: they neither sow nor reap nor gather into barns, and yet your heavenly Father feeds them. Are you not of more value than they?

27 And which of you by being anxious can add one cubit to his span of life?

28 And why are you anxious about clothing? Consider the lilies of the field, how they grow; they neither toil nor spin;

29 yet I tell you, even Solomon in all his glory was not arrayed like one of these.

30 But if God so clothes the grass of the field, which today is alive and tomorrow is thrown into the oven, will he not much more clothe you, O men of little faith?

31 Therefore do not be anxious, saying, 'What shall we eat?' or 'What shall we drink?' or 'What shall we wear?'

32 For the Gentiles seek all these things; and your heavenly Father knows that you need them all.

33 But seek first his kingdom and his righteousness, and all these things shall be yours as well.

34 Therefore do not be anxious about tomorrow, for tomorrow will be anxious for itself. Let the day's own trouble be sufficient for the day."

When I read those passages something in me changed. God's word can do the same for you! It was as if God had pulled up a chair at my table and was speaking face-to-face with me. It doesn't matter what the problem is, He is always ready to help. Maybe your mammon is work, addiction, anger, or anxiety. He does this if we just take the time to listen. If you are a worrier, don't let the enemy steal your peace. Stay in today's grace. Tomorrow's grace is not yet provided. As time passed the situation did as well.

There were more of those scary days, but God was so good that every time we got frightened He would put that verse in front of us. Hard days are sure to come; be ready for them by keeping God's word in your heart. This is the best advice I could ever share with you. Pray together and let God start multiplying grace in your marriage – which brings me to another point about sharing faith in a marriage.

How many of you reading this have a spouse that isn't where you want them to be spiritually? Have you tried everything you know except knocking them out with a frying pan and dragging them to church? If this is your experience, maybe I can help you a bit with my story.

As I said earlier, we always went to church. Maybe with a hangover at times, but we were there every Sunday morning. Around the time that the financial crisis happened, I started looking into other resources for my spiritual growth. I was on to something good. Besides Renew, and Bible Study Fellowship, I was also attending a Charismatic prayer group. My soul was being awakened and I loved it. While in Renew we began hearing about the Cursillo Movement. Cursillo is a program in the Catholic Church designed to bring those involved into a closer walk with the Lord.

I was on a quest for anything that God had to offer; Kenny . . . not so much! This began a period of unequal yoking and a time when I was acting as if I was the third person of the Blessed Trinity – you know: the Holy Spirit! I wanted Kenny to share in this wonderful experience of God with me. I tried to get him to do everything I was doing. He did enjoy Renew, but he just wasn't ready for my prayer group or Cursillo. At times he would attend things with me, but he didn't really want to go and when he did, it made for some miserable experiences.

It doesn't have to be a spouse you want this awakening for; maybe it's your children or a very close friend. The things that I have to say about being the Holy Spirit for someone applies to any person you want to come alive in Christ.

So my first piece of advice is BACK OFF! You are not the Holy Spirit. Your job is to pray, pray and pray some more. You are to lead by example; you ask God to give you opportunities. You pray that others to whom they will listen will come into the path of those you love and want to bring closer to God. God has a plan to reach each person on this earth and the plan is tailor-made for each of us. Guess what? God heard my heart and used a man that wasn't a holier-than-thou kind of man.

Johnnie was Kenny's softball coach for the Knights of Columbus softball team. He was a fun-loving guy who liked to drink a little wine and didn't preach, but led by example. If you attended a Cursillo, you had to have a sponsor and Johnnie was Kenny's and for that I will ever be grateful. After a lot of praying and a lot of begging Kenny did attend a Cursillo weekend. I believe Kenny thought if Johnnie can be a part of this retreat thing and still be real, maybe it's not so bad.

Cursillo is a wonderful tool to evangelize Catholics in the Catholic church. It had a profound effect on Kenny. The night he came home from the weekend he came in the door and started crying. He had been so touched by the Lord that his emotions were all over the place. I was very happy and could see that my prayers were being answered. I wish I could say that this was the end of me backing off and that we instantly became a couple who shared our faith the same, but it wasn't that way. I continued to grow at a faster pace and although Kenny had experienced growth, he wasn't where I was.

In fact, I was that person that needs locking up for a while after the Lord gets them. I was a bit out of balance and needed some tempering. Kenny didn't know how to handle me. I think he was afraid that I was going to change too much and that scared him. There were times that I left to go "churchin" when I should have stayed home. I just had an unquenchable thirst for all things of God and knew this was the faith-glue we needed.

Things got rough between us. He would say things like: "You should have been a nun; This is too much religion; I don't want to talk about this anymore." This would hurt me terribly. I did pray for him but I still tried to be in control. As I let go and quit pushing, Kenny came around. This took years. Kenny changed, and so did I.

Prayer usually changes us as much as the person we are praying for if we truly are seeking God's will. God began to show me areas that I needed to work on and as I became more loving and accepting of where Kenny was in his journey, Kenny's heart became more pliable to the Holy Spirit. The very things that I saw in him that needed change were only mirrored back to me. It's easy to recognize a familiar spirit in another.

Why do you see the speck that is in your brother's eye,
but do not notice the log that is in your own eye?

—Matthew 7:3

All along when I was seeking growth in Kenny, it was happening day by day in small ways, and I couldn't see it. I was wanting a lightning bolt, but God was gently chipping away, bit by bit. When Kenny did start to grow at his pace and in God's plan, the results were awesome. All the things I had told him over those years started coming back to me from his mouth. He would say: "Why are you worrying about that, you told me this or that." We dealt with a lot over 15 years as we struggled to get evenly yoked in our faith.

Kenny is absolutely a wonderful, faithful, Catholic man. He has been faithful to me, has been open to life, and loves his family with fierce passion. He is a "braveheart" when it comes to all of us. Kenny went on to serve on many Cursillo teams (over a period of about ten years) giving talks, washing dishes, helping with the facilities position and ended up serving as the Rector over one weekend. When God does something, He does it big!

Kenny has kept a holy hour at 3 a.m. every Sunday for more than 20 years. He loves going to see Jesus every week. He is the one that asks me to be sure and sign up for our annual Charismatic Conference because he loves going to it. If he says the he doesn't want to go to something with me at church, I accept it because it's his decision, not mine. We have so much more peace with this approach.

He supports me so very faithfully in all my ministries. He is a covering for me when I am in a discernment period over ministry decisions. Even if I don't agree with him in what he says after we have talked about it, I try to do as he asks because he is the head of our home. I've learned this keeps me out of trouble in saying yes to things I shouldn't.

Even though I might be the one on the front lines in different ministries, I tell him all the time, and I mean it, his role as the best supporter of me and the time he sacrifices from my being away are credited in his spiritual bank account. Plus I know he is praying for me!

If you take anything from this chapter about marriage, let it be that you must pray together and have God as the center of your marriage. Prayer in marriage is a must if you are to survive. God is able to go above and beyond your needs!

Now to him who by the power at work within us is able
to do far more abundantly than all that we ask or think,
—Ephesians 3:20

THE ROMAN CATHOLIC CHURCH has survived for more than 2,000 years and has given wisdom to its members for that long. Yes, she has had some dark times, but it is the oldest Christian church and has stood the test of time. One area where the church has guided married couples, is in the area of natural family planning and fertility issues. For many couples, natural family planning, referred to as NFP, is a hard teaching to follow; but there are many who use this method and know the benefits this can bring to a marriage. First of all, the couple must pray and understand the reasons behind the teaching of the church. What I am going to share is only my experience and I think it is worth sharing. NFP requires prayer, charity, and grace.

When I was a young teenager in 1968, Pope Paul VI came out with Humanae Vitae (Of Human Life). The world, but especially the United States, was undergoing a major shift in many areas. Women's rights movement, bra burning, free love, abortion, and the birth control pill (introduced in 1960) were some areas of concern. My uninformed conscience jumped on the bandwagon with the rest of the free thinkers and thought how can birth control be wrong? (I will say that I always have been, and will always be, against abortion.) Surely God understands that family size must be limited at times, and how can IVF be wrong or other methods of fertility treatments? Didn't the church say to be fruitful and multiply?

The problem with this kind of thinking is that we think that we are always the exception to the rule. I am not in any way standing in judgment of you or your decisions, this is only my story and how I came to see the beauty of the church's teaching. It is my observation that as methods of birth control and abortion became readily available, sexual promiscuity and the plague of STD's increased. Was this entirely due to increased sexual activity? In my opinion yes, but there's also a scientific proven medical reason. Due to the hormones, the mucous in the cervical area thickens and becomes a breeding ground for STD's to grow.

I want to be brutally honest and transparent as I share our journey with contraception in our marriage. Deep in my soul, I always knew what the church's stance was on contraception and using birth control always left me feeling guilty and shameful. It was a struggle that I dealt with almost daily. I wanted to follow the church's teaching but it was very hard. I would take the pill, then get off of it.

While taking it, I would notice effects that my body experienced from the hormones; weight gain, low sex drive, loss of romance, headaches and at times, I felt like I was being used. Now, I don't think Kenny ever meant to use me, but that's what was in my head. Some priests would say, follow your conscience, others would definitely preach against birth control, leaving me confused at times.

As my relationship with the Lord increased, I began to become more convicted that my root problem was a lack of trust in God. I was scared to have a lot of children and so I yo-yoed back and forth. Each time I was getting closer to the truth, not because the church said so, but because I felt the Holy Spirit convicting me personally. I think I was afraid to read and educate myself because I knew it would call me into accountability and it would lead to a more sacrificial lifestyle. Plus I knew Kenny had to get on the same page as me and I wasn't sure how he would feel. I began to study literature on NFP and the more I read, the more beautiful the teaching became. It was at a Charismatic Conference that I had picked up the literature that was transformative. I was reading how the pill works and my heart began to weep because I realized that I, who was so against abortion, could have possibly aborted one of my own children. I was guilty and the judgment I had about other people came right back at me.

You see, the pill can prevent pregnancy in three ways. It can stop ovulation (but sometimes doesn't); it dries up the mucous fluid that helps the sperm travel to the egg thus making it more difficult to reach the egg; and if those two things fail and the egg and sperm unite, it makes the lining of the uterus hostile for the egg that got fertilized to implant and in that case, you have caused an abortion. Yes, it was sickening to me to think this could have happened.

Haven't you heard of women taking the pill, who in fact got pregnant? These were the blessed babies that survived against all odds. Do your own research; pregnancy starts at fertilization, not implantation. Only in recent years has there been a push to change the language of when a baby is a baby. Is it at the moment of conception or implantation in the womb? Your pregnancy due date is figured from your date of fertilization, not implantation. This is true and has always been true.

In my opinion it is a way to keep from supporting the truth about birth control pills causing chemical abortion. In this age of instant information, you can find so many opinions due to so much information available on the internet these days. Just because it's on the information highway of the internet doesn't mean it's truth. My prayer and desire for you is to thoroughly research both sides, be open to the truth and use reliable sources. If you aren't fully onboard for NFP, why not take slow steps toward getting there. There are much less harmful ways to prevent pregnancy than taking the pill. Kenny and I talked and made the decision we had to quit contraception drugs. We continued to study and read about

NFP which, if practiced faithfully, can be just as effective as the birth control pill.

Can a person use NFP and still miss the mark on what the church teaches? I believe the answer is yes. Couples should be open to life. There should be serious reasons for limiting the number of children in a family. Using NFP just for the sake of not wanting more children can be sinful if done in the wrong spirit. Some examples would be wanting more material goods that are not necessary such as boats, fancy cars, second homes, or not wanting to be bothered with the day-to-day care of children.

Surrendering to God's will in your life takes daily crucifixions. Doing the right thing is not always easy. We had three children at this point in our marriage. I was working full time trying to help keep us above water with the demands of raising a family. My involvement in different ministries at church had grown. I loved serving my family and the Lord. There were times that I think I forgot that my family was my first priority.

Somehow I got in my head that, because I was serving God, limiting my family size was justified. Kenny wanted another baby but I was reluctant. In my heart, I knew my family wasn't complete but I couldn't see myself with another baby and the demands that would make on me. I just wasn't sure I wanted to offer up my body one more time. God is gentle but persistent and so was my husband. I want to also say that from age 20, my husband always wanted children. That is rare to me especially in this day and time. So back to my story.

The slow death to my will began in a car full of ladies on the way to the Charismatic conference in New Orleans in 1988. As I stated before, we were convicted to stop using artificial means to prevent pregnancy.

On the way to New Orleans my girlfriends and I talked about a lot of issues. We all had deep needs that we hoped would get met at the conference. We prayed and shared for the nine-hour ride. God was working in a powerful way with each of us.

I told the women about how I knew God was calling a baby forth and how Kenny had been wanting another child. It wasn't that I didn't want a baby, I was just scared of all the what ifs. Working full time and running a household of five was two full-time jobs. How could I possibly take on another person to care for? There would be sleepless nights, surrendering some of my time to ministries, the other three children that I already had would get less from me; the list was a mile long, but my heart did yearn for another baby.

The focus was all about my will, not God's. My girlfriends prayed in the car for me to be able to surrender. I was scared, but I was gaining more courage by the hour. The conference was awesome. Attendees were given opportunities for breakout sessions during the day. My eyes and heart were drawn to one session that was called something like "Christian Womanhood."

When I walked into the room for that session I began to cry; first interiorly and then outwardly as I heard this mother of eight tell her story about surrendering her will to have children. It was my story. I was thinking: "Lord you set me up on this one!" As I listened and prayed I heard God interiorly say: "You have tried to surrender all parts of your life, why don't you surrender your uterus to me as well?" The Holy Spirit had touched my inner being and I felt God's peace the rest of the weekend and all the way home.

We got home around midnight after the conference. Kenny was already asleep but woke up to me saying to him that I wanted to have another baby. He didn't have to think about it. His response was elation and surprise. Only God could orchestrate the fact that I was ovulating that day. Had the circumstances been different, I might have crept back into fear instead of faith and the outcome would not have been so wonderful! When we made love, I knew without a doubt that God was creating life at that very moment. It was the most powerful experience of God that I have ever had to this day. No words can accurately describe the emotions that I felt.

The next morning when I woke up, I turned the page on my morning devotional calendar and this was the verse for that day:

Lo, sons are a heritage from the Lord, the fruit of the womb a reward. 4 Like arrows in the hand of a warrior are the sons of one's youth. 5 Happy is the man who has his quiver full of them! He shall not be put to shame when he speaks with his enemies in the gate.

—Psalm 127:3-5

It didn't say that children are a curse or a burden. . . this is the world's opinion. When I read these verses, I knew God was giving me a confirmation. He was giving me a word of hope to hold onto. I knew without a doubt that I was pregnant and when I got to work, as an act of faith, I told my employees that I was in fact pregnant. They were surprised when I told them I was only about 24 hours into the gestational period. I wanted everyone to know that this baby was planned and very much wanted and not a mistake as some would want to believe.

Nine months later our sweet daughter Abbey Marie was born. We couldn't imagine life without her. Her name means her father's joy and it fits her so well. God the Father, her earthly daddy Kenny, and I all have been blessed by her life. I want to conclude that she is now 28 and none of the things that I was afraid about came to be.

I have always known that we made the right decision 28 years ago, but as I was rocking my ninth grandchild, Abbey and Ben's baby Benjamin, a flood of grace came over me. This beautiful newborn grandson was giving me a joy that I would have never known if I had not surrendered to God's will many years ago. Each time I look at Benjamin, I just say "thank you, God, for more love in my life."

Looking back, I wonder if there were more Abbey's that we were called to have but were too fearful. What is it that God is asking you to surrender in your life, in your marriage? Be not afraid!!

For some who are reading this, your struggle might be just the opposite. You want a baby so much but you are suffering from infertility issues. I've walked down that road in my family as well.

You are struggling with the Catholic Church's teaching on unacceptable fertility treatments. You carry tremendous pain in your heart that longs for a baby and you need the grace to follow the teachings of the church. There are those of you that haven't married and have come to realize that you are at an age that you cannot get pregnant anymore. All of these issues require daily crucifixions and surrendering to God's will.

Maybe you've had an abortion and carry tremendous pain. Whatever the issue you are dealing with, take it to the Lord in prayer. I believe that God rewards obedience and I know that His grace is sufficient to get us through each day.

After 44 years of marriage, I can say that almost everything we worried so much about never came to be.

Couples who do not have children can parent others in a way that a couple with children cannot. These couples have the time to impart faith, to birth Jesus in those they encounter. God works uniquely in each of our lives.

When a marriage is gifted with children it is, to me, one of the biggest blessings you will ever experience. It doesn't matter how those children come into your lives, they are a gift.

Each one of our four children are uniquely special and have brought us so much joy, but having children can stretch you to the limits of patience, finances, heartaches, and trust. Couples must work as a team to raise a family and since there are two of you, it stands to reason that you will probably disagree at times. This happens because you were parented by different sets of parents and we tend to parent as we were parented. Another factor is that a woman and man approach life from different views simply because of their gender.

As I look back after raising my family, I can say the some of our biggest disagreements were over the stresses of having children. It is in those stresses that you must learn to reach out to God and other strong couples who have undergone trials and made it through to the other side. There are so many issues in raising a family today; some of them are addictions, sexual promiscuity, self-entitlement, safety concerns such as predators and internet enticements, violence in schools, blended families; the list is long. Prayer is the key to survival.

There are so many issues in a marriage. I have only touched on what I believe are two very important things: faith and children or even the lack of children. These are two areas that God used to grow us as a couple and individually. With faith in a marriage, the struggles are easier to handle.

As I bring this chapter to a close, I part with some wisdom from being married as long as we've been married. Don't forget to go on dates with your husband. Always make special time for your spouse. We have a standing date every Thursday night. First we go to Mass and then we go out to eat and sometimes a movie.

Besides date night, it takes unconditional love in a marriage. One that is mirrored in the image of Christ. One that is self-donating, and sacrificial. It takes two people who are scholars in forgiveness. I realize that I don't have to be right all the time. I realize that I am a faulted human who contributes my fair share of junk daily. I have become keenly aware of how God loves me through my husband and children. I realize that God is using this wonderful husband of mine to cause growth in my own faith life.

Marriage is a covenant which is so very different from a contract. A contract has stipulations that if broken can nullify the contract. A covenant, as God demonstrated, is a life for a life; it is to be lawfully wedded, to have and to hold, from this day forward, for better, for worse, for richer, for poorer, in sickness and in health, until death do us part.

What has touched you in this chapter and if change is needed, how might it be implemented? How is God calling you to be more generous with those that you love?

CHAPTER 4
PRAYING: AN ACT OF FAITH

Prayer: what is it and how do you do it? I certainly don't have all the answers but I have learned a few things over the years. I also know that, as a spiritual director, one of the most common things people tell me is that their prayer is dry and that they want to hear God. I have experienced these same thoughts and feelings myself and have concluded that if you want to get better at praying, you just have to do it.

Please allow me to share some ways that I have grown in prayer and, hopefully, it will open the doorway to grace for you. In my first chapter I shared how God used my experiences on the farm to teach me who He was and about His character. I also shared about having the privilege to attend Catholic schools for twelve years. This groundwork laid in my childhood gave me a base to build on. It is only by the grace of God, through the power of the Holy Spirit, that we can even begin to pray. As a child, my prayer was mostly rote prayer and prayer of petition. I don't remember being told to have a relationship with God. I know it was implied, but I just didn't get that part.

I was given an arsenal of prayer to draw upon. My Catholic faith gives me a rich tradition to draw from when my heart just can't articulate what's in my head. Rote prayer is always beneficial when in a crisis. Praying the rosary and meditating on the mysteries of Christ's life is one example of a way to stay connected when we just don't have the words ourselves, but it isn't the only way to pray. Sometimes I think that rote prayer can get us in the habit of just going through the motions without giving much thought to what we are saying. As I grew older and life began to present itself in challenging ways, I began to realize that there had to be more in being a good Catholic Christian and my prayer life was challenged to go deeper.

The more I studied God's word, the more I saw the power of God and how He desires intimacy with each of us. When troubles come and our prayer life is weak, we realize that we better pray because we need God's help. This is usually how God begins to grow us in prayer; a need arises, a situation beyond our control happens, we experience the loss of a loved one and we fall on our knees and begin to beg or bargain. This is how it started with me, at the kitchen table that Sunday morning many years ago. If I pray long enough or pray well enough, God will love me and help me.

My prayer life and faith then was more like a child who believes in Santa Claus. Richard Rohr states this so well. "Without recognizing it, many people have an operative image of God as Santa Claus. He's "making a list and checking it twice, gonna find out who's naughty or nice." He rewards the good kids with toys (heaven) and punishes the bad kids with lumps of coal (hell). If you don't have a mature spirituality or an honest inner prayer life, you'll end up with a Santa Claus god, and the Gospel becomes a cheap novel of reward and punishment. That's not the great Good News! An infinitely loving God is capable of so much more than such a simplistic trade off or buy out."

Even though I felt like I was doing something to bring about the answer to my prayer, in reality, it all depended upon God. As I look back, my prayer was making a difference. Not only was it an act of faith, it was beginning to change me. God's word says to ask, seek, and knock, and I was certainly doing more than knocking; I was beating on the door.

> **"Ask and it will be given to you; seek and you will find; knock and the door will be opened to you.**

—Matthew 7:7

In reading God's word I began to know what God says about prayer. He says: *Have no anxiety about anything, but in everything by prayer and supplication with thanksgiving let your requests be made known to God. 7 And the peace of God, which passes all understanding, will keep your hearts and your minds in Christ Jesus.* **- Philippians 4:6-7**

My prayer life then was also like a fast food restaurant. I would pull up to the drive through window, place my order and be on my way. I might remember throughout the day to ask again, but I was always doing all the talking and it never occurred to me to stop and listen. I also thought that if I did prayer the "right" way I would certainly get my answer. My prayer was mostly all in my head and not from my heart.

The more I prayed, the more my prayer began to change. I began to actually think about what I was asking. It occurred to me that maybe I wasn't always asking what was the best thing for that particular situation. This change in praying started as I began to hang around people who had a personal relationship with Jesus and who could teach me by example.

As I mentioned earlier, I started going to a charismatic prayer group. Week after week, I was drawn to this group. The people were awesome, but it was the Holy Spirit wooing me. We would have praise and worship, quiet reflection, teaching and intercessory prayer. I believe it was here that I started knowing the Holy

Spirit. I was fascinated by the gifts of the Holy Spirit operating in the group. I was never afraid; I only wanted to grow and tap into this power source I was learning about. I had the Holy Spirit in me, I just had never stirred up those graces. I was very open and wanted to experience a baptism in the Holy Spirit. My attitude was: Give me all you got Lord. Yes, I was baptized, but this was my way of saying as an adult, I want you Jesus, I want you Papa, I want you Holy Spirit.

I sat under the teaching of a precious lady whom I consider my spiritual mother. Pat was always there for me. She always had just the right words or the right book to read and I devoured everything in my path. I wanted any gift the Lord wanted to give me. There were many times each week that I went up for prayer. Each time, the Lord was doing something in me. My heart would ache for more of God each week. Couple this with Bible Study Fellowship, and Renew and I was like a log on a fire that was starting to blaze.

The moment that I can say without a doubt that the Holy Spirit touched me was a healing service on March 2, 1986, in Barton Coliseum where the Rev. Ralph Di Orio was the presenter. There were many manifestations of the power of God happening all around me. There was an opportunity to go forward for prayer and I couldn't wait. My heart was beating fast and I was starting to feel as if I was the only person in the whole coliseum.

As the priest laid hands on me, I felt this immense peace and love come over me. I felt as if I were floating. My body was swaying back and forth and in a crowd of over 7,000 people, there was total silence around me. As I walked away, I knew something very special had happened to me. Kenny was with me at the healing service. I asked him if he had experienced the same things as me. He had not, but I am certain he was the recipient of grace that day. Maybe that encounter with God was what gave him the fortitude to attend that Cursillo weekend some years later.

When I got home after the healing service, I couldn't sleep because I was determined I was going to read the Bible from cover to cover that night. Let me just say that didn't go quite as planned because when I got to who begot who, I quickly got lost. On a side note, if you are beginning to read scripture for the first time, I suggest you start in the Gospels. I also suggest that you purchase a journal and write down what moves you as you read and pray. Journaling takes some discipline but it is a proven way to see what God is trying to say to you and where He might be leading you. Most of the contents of this book were first written in my prayer journal.

EVEN THOUGH I DIDN'T read my Bible from cover to cover at that time, a thirst for God's holy word was given to me and a new awareness of the power of the Holy Spirit as well. I continued to attend prayer group. Each week the Lord added grace upon my nature and I couldn't wait to go back the next week.

Wow! Little did I know how my love for God and his people was going to grow! The Lord's exciting journey for me was about to begin or should I say continue (for He had never left me, it was me that took wrong turns at times) with great excitement. I had been awakened.

> *But you shall receive power when the Holy Spirit*
> *has come upon you; and you shall be my witnesses in*
> *Jerusalem and in all Judea and Samar'ia and to the end*
> *of the earth."*

> **—Acts 1:8**

Are you reading this thinking I need some fresh fire from the Lord? Maybe you have been following him all along and you just need a booster shot. Please stop here and sit in silence before the Lord with the desire of your heart.

*For the Lord God is a sun and shield: he bestows favor
and honor. No good thing does the Lord withhold from
those who walk uprightly.*

—Psalm 84:11

Papa wants to bless you!

ALTHOUGH I AM CATHOLIC, and I had never crossed over denominational lines before, attending Bible Study Fellowship was a great grace-filled time in my life. If there was a local Catholic Bible study in my area at that time, I was unaware of it. (There are wonderful Bible studies within the Catholic church; one of them is from my home diocese and it's called Little Rock Scripture Study. We just didn't have it at my church at that time) I was invited to attend BSF and I prayed about it and answered the call.

Attending this particular Bible study was a bit of a challenge because it meant I had to give up a half day of work each week. In faith, I took the chance. Each week the Lord blessed me with new insight about Him. I finally had an organized way to read scripture and it was effective in my life. I gleaned many things from my five and a half years in BSF.

Two particular teachings that went deep into my soul are to pray specifically, with faith in God that He will answer, and the necessity of being a witness and evangelizing in your everyday environment. Being a witness in my environment also dove-tailed with what I had learned during my Cursillo weekend. Let me share two particular verses and how they played out in my life at that time.

*Therefore I tell you, whatever you ask for in prayer,
believe that you have received it, and it will be yours.*

—1 John 5:14

Kenny and I always went floating on the Buffalo River in Arkansas each spring. It is beautiful there and God's creativity is all around you. Due to the incline on the upper part of the river, the Buffalo has to be floated in spring to keep from doing a lot of paddling or dragging your canoe. This particular year, Arkansas was having a springtime drought. We hadn't had any rain to speak of and our float trip was looking like it wasn't going to happen.

My faith was being put to a test. It not only required faith, but testimony to God's ability to answer prayer. You've probably heard people speak of the honeymoon time with our Lord. It's a time usually when your love relationship with God is new and things go pretty much the way you pray. Our Lord knows we need to be gently brought along and this is one of those examples of asking and receiving in my honeymoon season.

I began to ask our Papa for rain. I also asked specifically as I was taught in BSF. My prayer was "Lord, please let it rain in Ponca, Arkansas, so we can have our float trip. Use this as an example of how you answer prayer, even in the small things." I prayed like this for several weeks, all along telling my clients in my salon that God was going to answer my prayer. Some laughed, some doubted, and some probably waited with curiosity.

The week came for our float trip and the circumstances were bleak. No rain, not even a promise of it. I was leaving work the night before we were to leave for our trip, praying and believing God when it started to sprinkle. I got excited and thought "Yeah, God". . . but the rain stopped as quickly as it started. I'll have to admit that I was beginning to get a bit doubtful and discouraged.

Some of my feelings about how God would answer my prayer were pure and some of them were ego driven. My ego didn't want to be embarrassed when I returned to work the following week if it hadn't rained.

That evening I was cooking supper and listening to the local weather with just a flicker of hope left, and the weather report became more depressing. The weatherman even made a comment that the Buffalo River was not floatable at this time and that it was really hurting the locals who depend on the floating season for income. My heart sank, but I uttered one more prayer "Come on Jesus, You can do this!"

The weather report was finished and the sportscaster was on when all of a sudden there was a break in the sports with the weatherman coming back on and a ticker tape running across the bottom of the screen saying that out of nowhere a hard rain was happening in Ponca and that the river would be floatable.

My heart burst with joy and I began to jump and praise the Lord. He had heard me and we would be able to float and I could go back to work on Tuesday and proclaim the good news. ***But let him ask in faith, with no doubting, for he who doubts is like a wave of the sea that is driven and tossed by the wind. -* James 1:6**

Do you need God to intervene in your life for a particular intention you have been praying for? Have faith in God and trust Him to work out that situation for the best. He is for you, not against you.

> *What then shall we say to this? If God is for us,*
> *who is against us?*
>
> **—Romans 8:31**

It wasn't so important that we got to float that weekend, the greater issue was that God wanted to increase my faith and show me the power of prayer. He also wanted to create income for the people in the river valley. He wanted to teach me to give Him glory after He answers prayers. **This is the confidence we have in approaching God: that if we ask anything according to his will, he hears us.**

STOP NOW FOR A PRAYERFUL PAUSE and bring your prayer intention to the Lord. Have faith that He hears you and will answer you in His time with His divine plan. God wants to change you as you pray. Many times the greatest fruit of our prayer is that we are changed. God is not Santa Claus, but a good Papa that knows how to give good gifts to his children.

If you then, though you are evil, know how to give good gifts to your children, how much more will your Father in heaven give the Holy Spirit to those who ask him!

—Luke 11:13

Lesson number two that was driven home to me in BSF was about witnessing for the Lord. Even though I had the powerful experience of the Holy Spirit at the healing service in 1986, I still carried a lot of fears and insecurities. As a hairdresser, I am given many opportunities to listen and share with my clients. Many times, my clients have serious issues that they are dealing with and could use a good word; not my word, but a word from the Lord. At this particular time in my life, I couldn't say the name of Jesus in public, let alone give my clients a word from the Lord. It was at BSF one morning that I heard this verse: *but whoever denies me before men, I also will deny before my Father who is in heaven.* - **Matthew 10:33**

My heart sank because this was me. I couldn't say the name of Jesus and I didn't want to be one of those people, but I also had a growing desire to serve the Lord. My life had come to a crossroad and I had to make a decision to pray for change. I didn't want Jesus to deny me before the Father and I didn't want to deny Jesus here on earth any longer. The verse kept playing over and over in my heart; not in my head.

The heart is where things really happen. **If you deny me before men, I will also deny you before the Father in heaven.** I quietly entered into the presence of Jesus that morning, and as I pondered the words in the silence of my heart I said a simple prayer: "Jesus, make me bold for you! Give me holy boldness." There, I said it. It was done. Little did I know where that simple prayer would take me. To my amazement, my feelings about Jesus started coming out of my mouth.

He who believes in me, as the scripture has said, ***Out of his heart shall flow rivers of living water.*** - **John 7:38**

I was like a well that had been primed and the water was flowing freely. The more that I witnessed, the easier it got. I wasn't fearful anymore and it didn't matter what others thought, I was on team Jesus now and we were claiming territory in the kingdom; first in my family, then in my workplace.

My beauty salon needed to be a place where Jesus was Lord and those who entered through the door knew it. Now, I must admit that I may not have always used the best approach. I needed tempering and grace and teaching that was nonjudgmental. As I became more vocal, I needed to have the faith to back up my words. There needed to be a detachment from what people thought or might have said about me either to my face or behind my back. There were days that this was hard.

As an evangelizer, you need a lot of charity to others and the grace to realize that God is working in different ways with different people. My approach was to share what God was doing with me and my family. I tried to be as transparent as possible as I shared. It wasn't my job to cookie cut them into my mold but to show how loving God is and how He wants to be in relationship with each of us. I haven't always thought in this way. In times past I felt everyone should think as I do. This new way of thinking is a grace that has been given over the years. As Jesus has transformed me, He has transformed my way of seeing to be more like He sees.

ONE DAY as I was sharing about God, I heard a lady in the back room of the salon say: "Now that she has seen the light, she won't stay Catholic much longer." My mind filled with anger and sadness. Why was my Catholic faith not good enough? I didn't retaliate with words but with my actions. I kept speaking of the love of God and I also realized that I was indirectly being challenged to know more about my Catholic faith. I should thank that lady because her remark only made me stronger in my faith; I had to take it for my own and not just be a Sunday Catholic. The good Lord used her to help me to become a vibrant Catholic Christian.

For every negative they say there is a positive if you want to call this next remark positive. Another lady, on a different day asked me where I went to church. I told her I was Catholic and she said: "Well you're not like the Catholics I know up north. You know scripture and you are a witness, and I think you are even saved."

I want to believe she was giving me a compliment in the best way she knew how. Her remark actually encouraged me. My reply to her was that there were a lot more Catholics just like me where I came from.

Be kind to one another, tenderhearted, forgiving one another, as God in Christ forgave you.

—Ephesians 4:32

9 Do not return evil for evil or reviling for reviling; but on the contrary bless, for to this you have been called, that you may obtain a blessing.
10 For "He that would love life and see good days, let him keep his tongue from evil and his lips from speaking guile;

—1 Peter 3:9-10

As I shared about the Lord, people began to open up to me more. This takes a good listening ear, respect and confidentiality. I had heard in Cursillo that we must be the leaven that changes the environment we are in and that we must bloom where we are planted. The environment of my salon began to really change. There was a peace as you entered the doors. My friends began to call my salon "Debbie's Hair and Prayer" because the salon became a place where Jesus was present and was even welcomed. Not only could I talk about him now; I was learning that I could also pray for these clients as they sat in my chair and God could meet them right there in the marketplace, but more about that is coming in another chapter.

These prayer experiences were in my early years of prayer. Prayer is not only doing but it's also a matter of being; it's a matter of knowledge moving from our heads to our heart through lived experiences. It has taken over 30 years to get me to the place I am today and I'm hopeful that in 30 more years, I will look back and see more growth in the way I pray.

In the end, it is all grace. We submit to God, hang out with Him, and the Holy Spirit brings the growth. Later on we will visit the prayer of silence and how the Lord brought me there.

Since I've shared with you about my growth in the salon, I want to move into my salon and how my growth as a Christian and prayer have transformed the environment.

CHAPTER 5
THE SALON: AKA DEBBIE'S HAIR AND PRAYER

I've been a hairdresser for more than 46 years now. I entered beauty school in 1972 while I was a senior in high school. I had aspirations to attend a local college, but my parents just couldn't see the benefit. They were both blessed with common sense and knew the benefits of living well within your means. However, they were not blessed with formal education: my mother went through eighth grade and my dad couldn't read. His schooling was not much past a few years. My parents couldn't see how a paper degree would serve me well; after all, they said: "You don't need to go to college, you're just going to get married and have a family and probably stay home with kids." Out of respect to them and a lack of valuing my opinion, I sought other avenues.

I went to the beauty salon with my mother on many occasions. I would watch the stylists and would imagine myself in their career. It seemed to me that it was a glamorous profession. Little did I know just how demanding this profession would be. As I thought about this career, I reasoned that you made women feel and look pretty and got to talk to people all day. I was inspired to think that

I might like to do this. I didn't really pray about it; I just made a decision that this was what I would do.

I brought it up to my parents and they didn't veto the idea. To them it was a doable idea. It was tangible and we were a blue -collar service-oriented type of family; so I enrolled in Jones Beauty School. I graduated in 1973 and by the fall, after graduating from high school, I was a licensed hairdresser living the glamorous life. Yeah, I stood on my feet for hours at a time, making modest money, and I listened to people and their life situations all day long.

I was only 18, so I had much learning to do about the outside appearance, but more importantly the inside beauty. God blessed me with a natural talent and personality to be a hairdresser. I wish I could say that I always gave God the credit for my skills, but I didn't. I thought it was all my own doing – hard work, continuing education, landing a job in the right salon in town. Yes, these things did help, but ultimately it was God using my natural gift and then collaboratively elevating that gift to become a supernatural gift. I'd like to take you on the journey toward God truly becoming the owner of my salon and the struggles I encountered along the way.

My first job was for the same lady who owned the beauty school I graduated from. I worked for Elizabeth for about eight years. I was happy there and was able to build a good clientele. At that time, this was THE salon to work at in my hometown, but God put a drive and passion in my heart to excel in all things. You could probably say that I have an overachiever type of personality.

My husband refers to me as "the drill" sometimes because when I get something in my head I go at it until the task is accomplished. My kids all call me Industrious D! My thoughts after working for someone for as long as I did was that if they could achieve success as a business owner, so could I. It was scary and exciting all at the same time. I actually did pray about my decision to open my own salon.

I'm not sure if I actually asked God if I should; I think it was more like, "Hey God, I'm going to do this, would you help me and give me your blessing?" Have you ever prayed that way? I know I have on more than one occasion. Looking back, what I thought was my inspiration was actually an inspiration from the Holy Spirit. I just didn't know it at the time! God was going to use me and it wasn't even on my radar!

My career as a salon owner was formed with the help of some professional people in the industry who steered me in the right direction. I followed their advice and I had the blessing of my husband as well. Kenny and I found the location after doing some research and did a complete remodel on a very run down building and transformed it into a premier salon that was one of the first of its kind in my city. Kenny, who was also self-employed at that time, decided he would go to work for someone else in order to ensure a stable income from at least one of us. Praise be to God, my business was off and running and God blessed me with a great business.

The early years of my business required me to learn about balance. I had a young family and a new business. Some days the stress was very difficult, but Kenny and I were a team and we kept going in a forward direction. After several years, Kenny and I could tell that my business was doing well and he could return to working for himself again. If you want to learn about divine providence and daily bread prayers, try having a household where both of you are self-employed. You will surely get your petition prayer down right if nothing else!

It was after being self-employed for about eight years that I began to hear about Bible Study Fellowship. This, along with other opportunities for spiritual growth, had a major impact on my everyday faith life. My business began to morph into something very different as I was growing in my faith. When I made my Cursillo weekend, the phrase to "Bloom where you're planted" was central to most of the talks I heard. I was committed to go back to my salon and bloom in every way possible. The verse about giving testimony to others about God had taken deep root in my heart.

> *But whosoever shall deny me before men, him will I also deny before my Father which is in heaven.*

—Matthew 10:33

It took many years for my salon to change into Debbie's Hair and Prayer. What I didn't know was that I was being transformed as well. For probably the first ten to fifteen years, I gave testimony about God, but that's about all; I still didn't have the courage to pray for people right then and there.

Praying for others at the moment takes a deep sense of knowing that the outcome all depends upon God and not the words that you say. Somehow, I felt that if I didn't say just the right formula, my prayers wouldn't work. Have you ever felt this way? Do you feel this way right now as you are reading this? My advice to you is to quit listening to the enemy. If he can keep you doubtful of the power of prayer, he has won power over you.

> *In their case the god of this world has blinded the minds of the unbelievers, to keep them from seeing the light of the gospel of the glory of Christ, who is the image of God.*

—2 Corinthians 4:4

THE BEST WAY to get comfortable with praying for people is to just keep doing it. As you pray, speak God's words in scripture. These are His words and He cannot go back on His words.

Now as my salon began to be a real transformed environment for Christ, the battle became a bit fiercer to stay competitive and keep employees happy and earning a good wage. Over the 37 years I have owned my own salon I have had many employees. I believe that some of them I helped, many of them helped me, and many of them were placed in my life for different reasons.

I tried my best to be a good boss, but I know at times, I failed. The pressure of running a business can be fierce at times and consequently that pressure can be transferred to others around you. When employees leave there's a change that happens and you have to respond to that change the best way you know how. This is where experience helps and most importantly seeking God's direction through prayer.

After many years of dealing with hiring and training new employees, I began to wear down. I began to question if I still wanted a business. My zeal for being the best salon and making the most money was waning because my heart was bending more toward wanting to be in full-time ministry. My husband and close friends would remind me that I was in ministry by being a light for Jesus in the marketplace. My clients always told me how they loved coming into the salon because they got a great service, but most importantly they loved coming into a Christian salon, which is very different from the norm. I was experiencing a conflicted inner man and I wasn't sure what to do with it.

Sometimes when God is wanting to bring you to a new place and you can't do it on your own, He allows situations that help bring about that change and they don't always feel good. I had one such occasion that started a series of events that I would like to share.

As I have mentioned before, Cursillo was a tremendous grace in our lives. So much so, that when there was a search for a new Executive Director, I felt that the Lord was calling me to that position. Kenny and I both knew it would be a tremendous stretch for our family of six. Our children were ages 7 through 19 at that time. Kenny and I were both self-employed and if I took the position, it would mean that I would have to give up two of my work days at the salon and trust that things would go well in my absence. The position meant I would have to travel into Little Rock two days a week as well as take off extra days when the actual retreat weekend was in progress. Kenny and I prayed earnestly and intently for a month. The desire and pull to do this became stronger for me each day. There were other applicants for the position so I knew that there would be opportunity to not be selected. This really gave me peace because at this time in my prayer life I knew that I better be doing this for the right reasons. The reasons couldn't be to inflate my ego, or for power or anything like that. Saying yes to this position would affect my family and my income because I would be giving up two days of work each week.

I felt my business could withstand me being gone those two days a week because I had reliable employees, so now it was up to the Lord and the interview team at the Diocese because Kenny and I had said yes to the call. I was hired and stayed in that position for almost six years. It was one of the most exciting and stretching times in my life! I loved being on the front lines bringing others to the love of God.

To everything there is a season and the time came that I knew that I was to leave the position as director of the Cursillo. It was very hard to leave because I had seen so much growth in myself and the movement, but I also was becoming very impatient with others around me. This was a sure sign that the Lord was wrestling with me to let go, but I just didn't know how. St Ignatius of Loyola says to be indifferent in all things. In other words to hold things loosely. Somehow I felt that my identity or worth was due to that position.

As I struggled to let go, and I did, what I was unaware of was that my employees were getting disgruntled with me. Some of the complaints were justified and others weren't. Long story short, when I came back to the salon things weren't as nice as I had left them. I was worn out from such intense ministry and I decided I needed a sabbatical from ministry for a while. That was short lived, however, when Penny Lord called and made an appointment for me to do her hair.

Many of you reading this will know who Bob and Penny Lord are. For those of you who don't, they were regulars on Eternal Word Television Network and were authors of many books and videos on the lives of the saints, but their most important work in my opinion was their book "Miracles of the Eucharist."

It was no time at all and I was being offered a job at The Holy Family Mission. I prayed and Kenny and I said yes. As I look back, I realized that I didn't discern this very well. While it was a great work in ministry, I had not stayed true to my original plan which was to take a sabbatical.

If I had been aware of the rules of St. Ignatius for discernment of spirits I would have known that this was probably a hook from the enemy camp. The evil angel will bring good things to you, but that doesn't mean they are good for you to do. He gets trickier as we grow in holiness. God doesn't waste anything. My time at Holy Family Mission was also a time of growth for me. I grew in new ways and I developed an even deeper love of the saints. I was given some great opportunities during my time there, and I was also shown the love of some very wonderful people; Bob, Penny, Brother Joseph and Luz.

I was only at Holy Family Mission for about two years because one day, two of my three employees quit on the same day. I was devastated. I had no recourse but to go back to my salon and try to salvage my business. It was a very painful time for me, but in spite of it all, God was beginning to really change my business to be HIS business. The circumstances forced me to let go yet once again and to enter into a new school of His training. I rebuilt my business and was content for the time being. A few more employees came and went, each time chipping away at my heart and stamina. I prayed for wisdom each time I hired a new person. I loved my profession, but I didn't enjoy the business side of it as much as I once did. One thing was for sure, the salon was becoming an oasis of grace for those who entered there.

Fast forward about six years and know that I found joy again as my niece came to work for me. We were together each day and she was a great help to me. I want to believe it was that way for both of us. I was approaching mid '50s and I was re-assessing what God wanted for my business and what we needed as a family.

Due to a change in pastors at my church, there was an opening for a business manager. It was a full-time position and something gnawed at my heart to look into applying for the job. One reason that I wanted to take this position was to get into full-time ministry, but there were other motives that probably weren't God inspired. They weren't wrong, just not reasons to make a decision from.

Remember, you have to be watchful for the hook of the enemy. The new pastor was a very close friend of our family for 30-plus years. Our church was not in the best place and I knew he needed a confidant to help him steer through the murky waters ahead. Kenny was not convinced that I should do this and neither were some of my friends, but they all gave me their support and blessings.

Many graces were given to me during this time that I call my pregnancy, birthing experience. Our good Lord was breaking me down in a good way. He wanted my full freedom, my liberty, my all. I did apply for the job and as I waited for word, I completely let go of any holds on my will with my salon. Leaving my business meant a drastic cut in my income, but I was willing to let go if it was God's will. There is one experience that I must share with you that happened during this process and this experience is the one that helped me to let go.

It was a winter day and there was a call for snow in the forecast. I went to daily Mass this particular morning, like I was accustomed to doing. I came out of church and there was a light snow beginning to fall. There was a special feeling in the air to me that morning. The song: "Mercy is falling, is falling, is falling," was going through my mind. I felt the presence of God in a profound way.

On snowy days, it is likely that people will cancel but I always try to go in to work and see what the Lord will provide that day. I had one client who was a very close friend that was due to come in and she was getting a rather lengthy service, so I called to see if she was going to try and make it. My goal was to work until the weather got too dicey.

My friend came in and we talked and prayed and shared life happenings together. The longer we talked the deeper the snow got. We were in a cocoon and the snow was the silk around us. To our amazement, we were the only ones in the shopping center and the snow had gotten pretty deep. There wasn't a tire mark or footprint anywhere to be seen. Ann had spoken of her now late husband and the battle they were having due to his cancer and I was talking about the possible closing of my salon. We cried and prayed as we shared our stories. There was a heavy feeling of seriousness in the air. We needed a little lightening up!

Ann had this idea that we should go outside and make snow angels. I can assure you that I hadn't done such a thing since I was a young girl. We bundled up and out the door we went. We laid down in the parking lot in the snow and began to spread our wings, up and down, up and down we went. As I was laying in the parking lot, I began to feel a true release of my will, a detachment, regarding my business. In the spreading of my wings up and down, peace and freedom took flight. We giggled like two school girls but I also cried as this experience came over me.

Have you ever felt the presence of God in such a palpable way? We stood up and admired our beautiful angels. I felt such inner freedom. As we faced the salon, we were standing in front of a mirrored glass store front. Ann said: "Look Debbie, let's take a picture of ourselves." We smiled at the glass and snapped a pretend picture that I carry close to my heart, and I will never lose sight of the image. That day was a touchstone moment in my life and my career. I truly let go and said God, it's really your business now, I'll stay or I'll close, please have your will here.

When you truly become unattached to an idea, a thing or a person the freedom you experience is unbelievable. I must say that I didn't even get an interview for the position at church and I was totally OK with that. In the waiting and praying, I knew it wasn't the right thing for me or for the church. God wanted me to stay where I was and to bloom where I was planted.

Are you in a place of struggle right now with a decision, a family member or a friend? I urge you to pray for detachment and the Lord's will and see what God can and will do. Why not stop right now and pray. Be still and wait on the Lord. Listen, obey and realize that our answers don't always come immediately.

This process of change in my salon took several years, but I can say it's the best thing that has ever happened concerning my business and ministry. I went from fretting about my income to totally depending upon divine providence. I also heard the Lord say to me that just because I had always done something one way didn't mean that I had to continue doing it that way forever. This word was concerning my hiring of new employees.

I was worn down and didn't have the energy to go through more training and the like. I realized that financially I was stable and able to be the only one in the salon and so that is what I did. It was a bit strange at first but I began to love the change.

I believe there were two main reasons that God spoke to me about making a change. One was for my own well-being and the other was to release the ministry of intercession and healing in my salon. This is what "Debbie's Hair and Prayer" was created to do.

I had been doing this for quite some time but this last change brought my salon ministry to a whole new level. I now had the opportunity to be with a client one-on-one, and that privacy began to allow for intimacy in prayer with my clients.

I want to interject that during the time prior to this change in my business, I had enrolled into a three-year program through my diocese to become an Ignatian Spiritual Director. I will speak more about that in another chapter but it is relevant here because my listening skills, as I stood behind my chair each day, had really grown and this new chapter in my life would bring about more change in the salon.

As I am writing this, it's been three years since I've made the decision and I don't regret it. I must tell one more piece in this story of the evolving "Debbie's Hair and Prayer." As I prayed about not hiring another employee, you could say I kept the door open to God's will. We should always be open to what he wants so as I spoke to Him about this matter I prayed a plan. It went something like this. "Lord, I'm not sure if I'm really hearing you correctly. I don't want to miss out on your plan. If you want me to have an employee or if you want someone else here, you're going to have to bring them to me!" Guess what? He did just that, but not before I had learned the lessons I needed at this time in my life.

I remained alone in the salon for over a year and then God began to move. He is always full of delightful surprises. My training as a Spiritual Director was coming to a close and it was time for me to begin to see those who wanted to avail the use of a spiritual director.

Discernment was needed to know how to go about implementing this ministry in my life and balancing my financial need to still work with giving up hours in my work week for spiritual direction. When God calls you to something specific, He will supply what you need in all areas; and He did this yet once again.

Remember how I told you that I had prayed that he would send someone to me if He wanted me to have someone there? He did just that and it was a remarkable situation I might add. To make a long story of several months short, I received a phone call from a past employee from 30 years earlier who was interested in speaking to me about the possibility of coming to work with me. I was her first employer right out of beauty school and had trained her.

It was a no brainer! Dana is a delightful, kind, and generous person who had matured into a wonderful hairstylist. She had sold her own salon and was looking for peace, freedom, and a less stressful environment to work. I didn't have to train her, I didn't have to wonder if she would be a good fit, and God was sending a bit of a financial help to offset the days that I would begin to have to give up to see people for spiritual direction. Not only did I benefit from this change but she did as well. Her schedule still allows me to have days at the salon alone if there are intimate needs with any of my clients, and she has a day alone as well.

I have to trust that God will work on their needs with my schedule by booking them when I am at work alone. Glory, glory hallelujah! He's something else. He's the real deal!

I want to take you now to some experiences that I've had as I've prayed with people both in the salon and in other circumstances. Some of these events have been miraculous in my eyes.

CHAPTER 6
CHARISMATIC AND CONTEMPLATIVE MARRY

Have you ever known an "all in" charismatic or a deeply contemplative person? Their spirituality is seemingly manifested in entirely different ways, yet both are equally good and both can be present in the same person. Charismatics express themselves with exuberant praise, dancing, ecstatic prayer language, and tend to be open to the spiritual gifts of the Holy Spirit through miracles, signs, and wonders with emphasis on a personal relationship with Jesus.

The contemplative person tends to savor quiet introspection with the Lord, deep listening, stillness in posture, deep gazing of one to the other. Contemplation is a grace and a gift and it produces the grace of transformation and oneness with God. Contemplation is a place where heart speaks to heart in silence. While both forms produce very similar fruits, the actual prayer is manifested in different ways.

For me, personally, the charismatic form of worship came first. My temperament is very outgoing, so being able to dance and praise the Lord was awesome to me. I was intrigued by the gifts of the spirit and I loved the idea of a charismatic prayer language.

There were so many times I didn't know how to pray for someone so the charismatic prayer language gave me peace.

I never doubted the authenticity of the renewal because I trusted the people who were showing me the way. I was also assured of the fact that the Catholic Charismatic Renewal was under the umbrella of the Holy Father and Mother Church. Learning about the gifts of the spirit and being open to the use of them set me on fire and gave me great confidence to be able to work in the name of Jesus. I have often explained the transformation that the renewal had within me to be like having a brand new car with all the bells and whistles but no idea of how to drive it or use all the extra features. Knowing about the fruits of the spirit helped me to drive the car, (my spirituality) with greater ease, and I was able to optimize those gifts for building up the body of Christ.

I experienced a freedom in worship that I had never known as well as a greater confidence in my ministries because I became so aware that I was only the conduit for the Spirit to move through. I spent many years going to weekly prayer meetings where I was instructed about the gifts and the fruits of the Holy Spirit. One example that I heard about the Holy Spirit is that we receive the Holy Spirit in baptism, and in confirmation we are given the opportunity to make a deeper commitment to the Holy Spirit. Compare the Holy Spirit as He relates to confirmation to liquid chocolate in a glass of milk. You pour the chocolate into the milk and it will settle on the bottom of the glass. The milk won't turn to chocolate milk until you stir it up. It's the same with us. The Holy Spirit is inside us, but we must stir up and fan into flame the Spirit in us!

There are fruits of the Holy Spirit and gifts of the Holy Spirit. It doesn't matter whether you are charismatic or contemplative, you should have the fruits and gifts operating within you.

"Just so, every good tree bears good fruit, and a rotten tree bears bad fruit. A good tree cannot bear bad fruit,

nor can a rotten tree bear good fruit. Every tree that does not bear good fruit will be cut down and thrown into the fire. So by their fruits you will know them."

—Matthew 7:17-20

THE FRUITS OF THE SPIRIT are: charity, generosity, joy, gentleness, peace, faithfulness, patience, modesty, kindness, self-control, goodness, and chastity. These fruits can be a good way to check your own life to see if they are operative within you. If you can't see these attributes within your daily life, it might be time to do some soul searching.

In the Book of Isaiah 11:2-3, the Gifts of the Holy Spirit are described. In the passage the gifts are considered ones that the Messiah would have possessed. Through Jesus, we also receive the Gifts of the Holy Spirit in the Sacrament of Confirmation. Wisdom helps us recognize the importance of others and the importance of keeping God central in our lives. Understanding is the ability to comprehend the meaning of God's message. Knowledge is the ability to think about and explore God's revelation and also to recognize that there are mysteries of faith beyond us. Counsel is the ability to see the best way to follow God's plan when we have choices that relate to him. Fortitude is the courage to do what one knows is right. Piety helps us pray to God in true devotion. Fear of the Lord is the feeling of amazement before God, who is all-present, and whose friendship we do not want to lose. There are other gifts mentioned in sacred scripture. In Romans 12:6-8 we hear of Prophecy, Serving, Teaching, Exhortation, Giving, Leadership, and Mercy. I Corinthians12:8-10 lists even more gifts; they are: Words of Wisdom, Word of Knowledge, Faith, gifts of Healing, Miracles, Prophecy, Discernment of Spirits, Tongues and Interpretation of Tongues. These gifts can even be expanded in many different directions. The main point is that these gifts are given to us for the building up of the body of Christ, the church.

It is possible that someone can get so caught up in the gifts that they forget the giver of the gifts, which is the Holy Spirit. I have witnessed that most people who are filled with the Holy Spirit have many of the gifts operating within them, but each person may have a gift or two that is their higher gift such as healing, or miracles. There are also times that I have seen someone given a gift for a particular time because it is needed in the body of Christ right then and there. We all have gifts but we must, like any gift, open it to use it. The more you use the gifts you are given the easier it is to put them into practice when they are needed.

It is my opinion that so many people are afraid to pray over someone or to give them a word of exhortation because they fear nothing will happen or that they might not say a "good" prayer or they might say something wrong. I say, get your eyes on Jesus, it all depends on Him. We do our part and leave the outcome to Him. My advice to grow in the Holy Spirit is to pray for an increase in the gifts and then to associate yourself with sound Christians who meet together on a regular basis and let them instruct you by word and deed.

I want to share something that happened many years after I received my baptism in the Holy Spirit. I was at our local prayer group one evening and on this particular night we had many college people there. They had been coming on a pretty regular basis. Some weeks some of them would want to receive the Baptism in the Holy Spirit. . . . They wanted their chocolate stirred up!

On this particular evening we had one young man express his desire to be prayed over. I was sitting next to him and there were probably twenty or more people all gathered around him. We started praying over him in our prayer language of tongues and English for about twenty minutes. God had truly touched him. I moved back to the place I had been sitting originally, which was away from him, and he asked who was sitting next to him. I told him it was me. He said, "Do you know that you kept saying thank you in Swahili?" He said that he kept hearing me say: "Asante" which translates to "thank you" in English! There were many people praying over him and for a long time. It would have been nearly impossible for him to isolate that one word from all that had been spoken. I knew immediately that he had heard me because I recognized that word as being a part of my prayer language for nearly thirty years.

When I returned home that evening after our prayer meeting was over, I googled the word "asante" to see if I could find the meaning of it. Sure enough, there it was. Asante means thank you when translated from Swahili to English.

The story of confirmation doesn't end here. If you still doubt charismatic prayer language, the Lord gave me another confirmation about that same word. It was several years later and I had forgotten about the whole meaning of that word. When you pray in tongues, it is not like you are thinking about what you are going to say next. The prayer language just flows freely and effortlessly. My friend and dynamic Catholic speaker Maria Vadia was visiting our home parish doing a mission. She was staying with me and I was with her each night for the week she was ministering to our church people. One night as I was praying over people with her, in between persons, she looked at me and said: "Do you know you are saying thank-you in Swahili?" I had a huge smile on my face and said we'll talk about it later.

You might be asking why she knew that word? The answer is that she goes to Africa every year to preach and teach. She told me there is a song they sing that goes: Asante, Asante, Asante, Jesus! Thank-you, thank-you, thank-you Jesus! It was the second time that someone had confirmed to me what I was saying. If you count the Google search, I actually had three confirmations! The gifts of the Holy Spirit are still operative today. God's word is as alive today as it was in the early church. We just have to be open to the gift.

We must also take time to study and pray to better understand the gifts and how they are to be used.

One other such example was in more recent years. I was in California at a Leaders Conference for Magnificat. Magnificat is a Catholic women's ministry that aims to help women come into a personal relationship with Jesus. We were at San Juan Capistrano in the Mission Basilica San Juan Capistrano waiting for Mass to begin. We were singing and praising God in ecstatic praise. Many women were singing in tongues and so was I. I absolutely love this type of worship.

As I was singing in tongues, a lady in the pew in front of me turned around when we had stopped and said, "You are speaking in Nahuatl." I wasn't sure what she was saying. "Are you saying Navajo," I asked? "No, it's pronounced Na-vo-tol. It is the language Our Lady of Guadalupe spoke to Juan Diego," she replied. She said I was crying out to the Father and the Mother.

After Mass was over, I was wondering if she had an interpretation of my tongues or if she actually knew the language. I looked for her in the crowd and couldn't find her. The rest of the day I looked for her but didn't see her anywhere. It wasn't until our evening Magnificat meal when I turned around to the table next to mine, that I saw her again. We were sitting back to back. What are the odds that God would place us strategically by each other, twice in the same day, in a crowd of 400 women?

"Excuse me," I said. "I've been wondering all day if you received a word of knowledge in the church about my prayer language, or do you speak the language?" She replied: "I studied this language some 40 years ago while I was in college. As I heard you speaking the words, I was immediately compelled to turn around and tell you what I was hearing. It wasn't like I thought about it for a while. It was totally spontaneous."

I have never doubted my prayer language, but if someone was a non-believer, maybe these two examples would help their unbelief.

Contemplative prayer was harder for me to practice and still is to this day. It requires stillness and deep listening and for someone who is a bit on the "busy" side it requires giving yourself permission to just waste time with the Lord. Contemplative prayer can even feel a bit as if you are being unproductive and in our world of production, that just doesn't seem to make sense. The truth is that it is in the stillness and deep listening that we learn how to be productive for the Lord.

Contemplation is a grace and we can't just will it into being, but when we are truly in a contemplative state of Divine Union, there is a sweetness that keeps you there and you really don't want to leave! It is a mirroring of God looking at you and the Jesus in you. Other names or descriptions would be a gaze of faith, or silent love. St. Teresa says: "Contemplative prayer [oración mental] in my opinion is nothing else than a close sharing between friends; it means taking time frequently to be alone with him who we know loves us. Contemplative prayer seeks him 'whom my soul loves'. It is Jesus, and in him, the Father. We seek him, because to desire him is always the beginning of love, and we seek him in that pure faith which causes us to be born of him and to live in him. In this inner prayer we can still meditate, but our attention is fixed on the Lord himself."

If you are a parent, think of the dialogue you have between you and your newborn baby. Eye to eye, heart to heart. No words are necessary or even possible from the baby, but you love them with every part of your being. Imagine that you are God the Father looking at your baby. As God the Father, you communicate through your expressions protection to the baby and your love, joy and admiration. Long before the baby can communicate to you, the gaze you share with your child is mirroring immense love. The baby sometimes tries to open his mouth to speak, but nothing comes out. They simply don't have adequate vocabulary to express their love back. I think this might just be how I explain contemplative communication between God and us.

For many years I would say to my Spiritual Director that I wanted to be a contemplative. I thought I could just will it and it would happen. My prayer life was hit and miss at this time, so to expect to sit with God in stillness when I couldn't even spend time quietly praying on a regular basis was mere love of an idea; but there was a desire and God gently wooed me along.

My pastor and very close friend Fr. John had gone on a silent retreat and he created a desire in me to do the same. He invited me to consider a silent retreat. I wanted to go but I actually was a bit afraid that I couldn't stand the silence or that I wouldn't do the retreat correctly. It wasn't until I attended my first silent retreat that I developed a greater understanding for less talking and more listening. It was only a three-day silent retreat, but I realized I could be quiet and that I wanted to give an eight-day silent retreat a try. So, the journey to interior quiet began. I want to interject that being quiet on the outside isn't nearly as hard as interior stillness and there is a big difference in the two. This retreat was the beginning of a new journey into contemplation.

There are different types of silent retreats. The type that I've experienced is silent in a strict sense; interior and exterior using the evocative contemplative method. Of course, there are no silent police at your retreat, looking for silence breakers, but the stiller and quieter you become, the more you receive. It was suggested that I not read any outside books or commentaries, stay off the phone, no texting, and have at least four hours of prayer in a 24-hour period, which can be broken up in any fashion. I was to read from my Bible the given passages from my spiritual director on the retreat, spend some time in meditation, and then journal about what the Lord gave me.

Other types of silent retreats can be less structured where you might read outside books, listen to sacred music, read commentaries, but for me total silence at different times in my life is just what the doctor ordered. There are also preached silent retreats where the participant stays silent, listens to a talk then leaves to meditate on that particular talk. Find the type that fits you best and then make a commitment to go. I believe at different times in your life different things will work. If you are involved in any type of ministry, it is of utmost importance to take time to get away from the noise of the world and get back to true north.

Allow me to share one small story from my first silent retreat. If you remember in my earlier chapter I spoke about how I was discerning whether to close my salon and go into ministry at my local church. When I attended my first silent retreat I was in discernment about this possible change. I went to see if God would speak directly to me about this; either through the director or His word. I heard from the Lord very powerfully on that three-day retreat and to this day, I can see how clearly he was speaking to me, but as they say, hindsight is 20-20!

As I look back I can say that in all honesty I was trying to make His words fit into my plan. Have you ever done this? You read His word or listen to a great speaker and you start trying to make your situation fit into what you've heard. In doing this, we really aren't open. We are merely manipulating the word to fit our needs. We must listen to God completely unattached and let go of our plan and wait on His.

One of the most powerful words he spoke to me on that retreat, along with very beautiful imagery, was that of a foundation of a home. Without going into word for word, He told me that my house was good but that he was going to add onto my foundation and shore it up, make it stronger. Of course because I was into making what I heard fit into my plan, I was sure He was saying that I was going to be changing course in my work career and moving into full-time ministry. Wouldn't you think if someone was going to "add" onto your foundation that could be a logical conclusion? Time is a great discerner. This "foundation" word was one the Lord wanted me to pray with until I understood what he was saying to me. I didn't know then that praying for a grace or with a word can take considerable time. We must wait on the Lord to see what He wants.

Many times I run ahead and say: "Come on Lord, follow me." In the deepest truth of my inner being, I know now that I must say that I was a bit too arrogant to believe that I might need some restructuring to be better fit for day-to-day life. I needed a bit of excavating in my inner man to continue to grow in holiness.

When the Lord speaks, He speaks in ways that you don't feel shamed or beat down, but in gentle truth. He affirmed to me that my house was good, but He also had told me that I needed to do some work on my house. As I look back, I can see clearly how he began the excavating and adding on to my foundation. I went through a very difficult time period, but I grew so very much during that time. Some of the inner walls of my house were torn completely down and then restructured to be stronger and more beautiful. If it were not for my spiritual director and the graces of God, I might not have made it through that season.

Contemplation is a lifelong journey. The silent retreats helped me to get to a place where I could be still and have a posture of interior silence before the Lord. My Charismatic prayer gives me the exuberance to praise the Lord with my whole being. These two types of spirituality are not either/or, but both/and. There is a time and place for both. I am thankful that I have been graced with both styles of prayer and everything in between. It was my openness to a deeper interior prayer and the Ignatian type of prayer that led me to become a spiritual director. I'll talk more about that later. Let me leave you with one more thought and teaching I received at my first eight-day silent retreat.

At this time in my journey, I was still very much more into charismatic prayer. The whole stillness and silence type of prayer was intriguing me as I tried to be obedient to the Spirit's call. The retreat was awesome because I wasn't so busy trying to do it "right" as I was at my first silent retreat. I had some profound movements in my prayer that I will share later, but what I want to say now is what I summarized to the others in the group as we closed the retreat. It's about crop rotation. Crop rotation refers to the practice of growing different types of crops (or none at all) in the same area over a sequence of seasons.

So what's wrong with planting the same crop in the same field season after season? As farmers thousands of years ago learned, several problems begin to creep up when you don't rotate crops. All of these problems can lead to decreased yields over the course of several years.

First, the land itself can become "tired" and less fertile. Our prayer life can become tired if we do the same thing over and over with no desire to grow and change. We become less fertile in our ministries because we need to rotate our prayer around a bit. Second, certain pests can reach levels that are hard to control when they learn to make a home near a field that always has the same type of crop. Satan the "pest" can find that tiredness we are experiencing and become a major pest to deal with. We get bored with prayer and just quit. To beat back our "pest" we must be diligent farmers of our souls, rotating our prayer crop regularly. When your life is busy, take time to sit quietly with God. When your prayers become routine, let God lead you toward a more active prayer life, one that gets you off your knees and out doing the work of the Lord in the world. Mixing it up will keep the "pest" from killing our crop.

Finally, land can be more susceptible to the forces of erosion if the same type of crop is planted repeatedly season after season. All types of prayer keep us from slowly losing our "ground." It is easy to develop deep gashes in our prayer life if we become stagnant by doing the same thing over and over again with no thought of what we are doing. We must take time to assess the content of our soil to see if we need to change the crop of prayer in our lives. Many times we don't have to quit anything; remember it's not either/or, but both/and. Develop the soil of your prayer life with all types of prayer.

Crop rotation helps mitigate each of these effects. Different types of plants require different types of nutrients from the soil, just as different types of prayer are called for at different times in our life. Changing crops routinely allows the land to remain fertile, since not all of the same nutrients are being used each season. For example, planting a legume, such as soybeans, helps to replenish necessary nitrogen in the soil. Various types of prayer can replenish our interior prayer life. Using your charismatic prayer language helps when you don't know how to pray. Sitting in silence before the Lord can help you to listen. In the past, not planting anything (also called leaving the field fallow) allowed the land to rest and replenish its nutrients. Some modern farmers will occasionally allow fields to lie fallow to rest, but crop rotation has helped to increase productivity by replacing fallow periods with growing different crops that replenish soil nutrients. One thing in our prayer life we don't want to do is to leave our field empty of prayer. We never go fallow of prayer, but we might rest our field in the sense of taking a sabbatical. We all need to rest; Jesus surely did!

Ask yourself this question: Am I restless with my prayer time? It is my experience that when this happens, our Lord is changing up our routine to break through to another dimension of intimacy with him. God is always offering a new doorway to grace. It's up to you to recognize who's knocking on the door and then to respond appropriately.

⇒++⇐

CHAPTER 7
THE CRUISE DIRECTOR CALL

The Lord has called me over and over through the course of my life. I've had calls to a career, marriage, motherhood, ministry, grandparenting, and mentoring, but most importantly He has called me to holiness. All of these individual calls have led me on the road to holiness. As you are reading this, I am sure God is calling you to something. What is He asking of you right now, and how will you respond? Your response will depend on many things; most importantly, in my opinion, is how well you are praying and listening, and how obedient you are. Oftentimes we need the help of a companion or guide on the journey to help us to discern or take the next step forward. A spiritual director could be just the help you need.

I've mentioned my silent retreats and the wonderful graces I've received from them. I probably would have never made it to a silent retreat if it were not for being in spiritual direction myself. I have had my spiritual director, Fr. Mark, for about seven years now. His patient contemplative listening with me has been priceless to my spiritual progress. Please allow me to share with you some of the graces I've received while in spiritual direction, graces from my retreats, and the call I received to become a spiritual director myself. By sharing with you what a silent retreat can be like, I pray it will give you the desire to make one yourself!

I believe that my initial call to be a spiritual director came at my second silent retreat at the Little Portion Retreat Center on More Mountain in the beautiful Ozark foothills of Arkansas. There was a desire in my heart to become a spiritual director, but it seemed impossible for me at this time in my life, so I just put it in the back of my mind. I knew there was no way that I could go to Creighton University for a month, three summers in a row, for the necessary training. Helping people is one of my gifts and I think this is one reason I was drawn to become a spiritual director. I had been seeing Fr. Mark, my director, for about a year and a half and had benefited so much from it. Seeking discernment to become a spiritual director was not even on my radar when I left for my eight-day retreat.

While attending that eight-day retreat, I was at a very broken, low place in my life. Kenny and I were barely able to keep our heads above water financially. Spending money on attending the retreat and missing work for seven days was near impossible for me to do, but I really needed help in so many areas. My inner spirit was so agitated and I was exhausted emotionally, spiritually, and physically. I was angry at Kenny for sure, (even though I shouldn't have been) and I didn't realize that I was angry at God too. I'm sure the Lord was thinking, finally I am going to get her still enough to minister to her!

There was one thought in my mind before going that gave me some solace. Since I couldn't be at the beach, maybe I could get in the car while there and sit in silence before the Lord at the Kings River. This river is a beautiful white water, canoe floating, trout fishing, river that was very close to the retreat center. This could be a vacation for me in some way. I figured if I was spending all that money, I should surely get something besides holiness out of it. Since I was aware that leaving the retreat center might not be permitted, I called my dear "brother" priest friend, Fr. John Marconi. He was the one who was putting on the retreat and I knew he would give me the proper advice, so I picked up the phone and called him. The conversation went something like this: "Hey, Fr. John, I was wondering if you think it would be OK if I leave the retreat center during the day and drive to the Kings River, which is very close by. I'll keep silent. I just would like to go be with God on the river's edge if I can." Silence for a bit and then: "Well it's your retreat and you can do whatever you want, but is that what the Lord is wanting? Could He be telling you that He wants you to come to **THE** KING'S RIVER?"

Now I am silent. . . . It took just a bit but I got it! "Oh the **KING'S** River. . . I'm going to be in the KING'S River . . . It's a river of grace!" His wisdom in handling that situation satisfied that desire to go to the river. What I knew now was that the KING's river was coming to Me! I would be flooded with graces as I interiorly flowed in the river. My dear friend Diane and I were in the car driving to the retreat when we got to the place where the Kings River crossed the highway, we got out and looked at it and took pictures there. This is where I believe my retreat actually started.

Diane and I do everything together when it comes to ministry. On a side note, people often get us confused and call us the wrong name. We were anxious a bit about the retreat and had been in the car talking for several hours when we started talking about who would be our retreat directors. I knew she would have Fr. John and I wouldn't because he and I were too close for him to be objective with me in that setting. I knew that there was a person coming from California who would have directees, (those who are in spiritual direction) so I assumed I would either have him or Fr. Mark, who would also be there. I also assumed that the California man was a priest. Diane slowly broke it to me that she had seen him at Mass and she was pretty sure he was a lay person. Diane told me that she didn't think that Fr. Mark was having directees.

This feeling of great disappointment came over me. I got quiet and angry! I needed a priest for my director. Here I was spending all this money to go, and I had all this stuff to deal with, and I was going to get a rookie lay person to help me sort through all this. I couldn't believe it. I felt that I had been tricked. Truth is, it was my own fault for not asking. How arrogant for me to think that I was special and deserved a priest.

When we got there and directors were assigned, I did get the layman Marco and I sulked up and went to the chapel and began crying. I cried for a long time. That evening when I met with Marco, I told him how I felt. I also told him to get me a priest because I needed to go to confession. Poor guy. . . here he was trying to get certified to be a director for an eight-day retreat and he had a brat throwing a fit right out of the gate. I bet he prayed really hard that night for help from the Lord to deal with the "crazy" woman he had been assigned.

After I went to confession, I went to the chapel and I literally cried so much that I fell asleep in the chapel on the floor under the altar. Yes, I did say under the altar. There were only about five of us attending the retreat, the two directors and two more priests who were supervising the directors, so we had the chapel very much to ourselves many times. I knew all of the people attending except one man and I really didn't care what he thought of me. I was in such a fragile state that literally being under the altar was comforting and safe for me.

I stayed under the altar for many hours during those eight days. As I looked at the tabernacle, in my mind's eye I could see that there was a river of life giving blood; the King's River flowing from the tabernacle that was flowing onto the altar and then dripping down on anyone who was near. I also got the imagery of being under the wings of the Lord God Almighty when I was under the altar. I was safe. I felt the presence of God in a palpable way.

1 He who dwells in the shelter of the Most High, who abides in the shadow of the Almighty,
2 will say to the LORD, "My refuge and my fortress; my God, in whom I trust."
3 For he will deliver you from the snare of the fowler and from the deadly pestilence;
4 he will cover you with his pinions, and under his wings you will find refuge; his faithfulness is a shield and buckler.
5 You will not fear the terror of the night, nor the arrow that flies by day,
6 nor the pestilence that stalks in darkness, nor the destruction that wastes at noonday.
7 A thousand may fall at your side, ten thousand at your right hand; but it will not come near you.
8 You will only look with your eyes and see the recompense of the wicked.
9 Because you have made the LORD your refuge, the Most High your habitation,
10 no evil shall befall you, no scourge come near your tent.
11 For he will give his angels charge of you to guard you in all your ways.
12 On their hands they will bear you up, lest you dash your foot against a stone.
13 You will tread on the lion and the adder, the young lion and the serpent you will trample under foot.
14 Because he cleaves to me in love, I will deliver him; I will protect him, because he knows my name.
15 When he calls to me, I will answer him; I will be with him in trouble, I will rescue him and honor him.
16 With long life I will satisfy him, and show him my salvation.

– Psalm 91

For now, I was safe and could really pour my heart out to the Lord.

I had beautiful imagery during that eight-day retreat. When I prayed, I got the feeling that Jesus and I were in a canoe. We were floating down the King's River. Sometimes he would let me help Him paddle and other times he told me to let him do all the work. We went through calm water and rough water. I had to trust Him while in the river. There were times we even went down the river in whitewater with no oars in the water.

I never felt scared in the canoe because Jesus was with me and had everything in control. The Holy Spirit was teaching me to trust Him in all things - when it is good and when it's not so good. If we could only remember that God is for us. He is always for our good! He is not out to punish us because we aren't good enough. If God allows us to suffer, it has to be for an ultimate good that we just don't always understand on this side of heaven.

As the retreat progressed and I was being taught by the Holy Spirit, the Lord kept me in the boat as we traveled down the King's River. It was probably day seven and I noticed I wasn't in the canoe any longer. I was on a cruise ship! I said: "Lord what are we doing here?" I can clearly see it still in my mind's eye. He said you are the cruise director on this ship. I was a bit surprised but He clearly told me that the reason I was the cruise director was because I could tell people about the excursions that were available. He made me aware that my life experiences had been different excursions and I had gotten the most out of the experiences that I had whether they were joyful or sorrowful. On excursions you see and experience many different things and when it's all over you ponder and savor the experiences.

A good cruise director doesn't choose excursions for the passenger, but merely lets them know what is available, and then they make their own decisions. The Lord brings different excursions to each of us and then we decide if we want to take the trip with Him.

As I prayed with this experience on my retreat and for months later, I began to see that this was the call from the Lord to become a Spiritual Director. It took four-and-a-half years for that vision to come to pass. I entered a program that our diocese was beginning and I discerned month after month until one day I had completed the course. The training I received was based on the teachings of St. Ignatius of Loyola. I now am a certified Ignatian Spiritual Director and I love sitting with my directees each month, listening to their stories and then, ever so gently, offering different excursion suggestions they might want to take with the Lord. This is all done with evocative, contemplative listening.

Could I take you back now to the retreat and share some more of the graces I received while being silent before the Lord? As I explained earlier, I had a lay person for my spiritual director. I met with my director each day for one hour and that was the only time I spoke. I only used my Bible and journal while there. I didn't listen to any Christian music or read any spiritual books or commentaries. It was just me and the Holy Spirit.

At the beginning of the retreat, I told the group of people in attendance that I was in a rough place. In a joking way, I told them that if they heard loud screams during the rest of the eight days, not to worry, it was me and that I really needed to let out a lot of pent up anxiety. Even though I said it in a joking manner, the truth was that I wanted to scream and I didn't really know who to scream at.

In my sharing in previous chapters, you probably have the picture of my nature as one of doing. There's much truth to that. As long as we are busy doing, it's easy to ignore what is going on in our inner self. We can just do, do, do and we forget to BE with the one who longs for us. For several days I was gleaning graces from the retreat, but again, I was busy making those graces fit into my agenda as the one who is busy doing.

It sometimes takes a few days to decompress on a silent retreat. Even though I was scared, tired, and spent a lot of time in the chapel, I also spent lots of time outdoors.

We had an awesome deck that overlooked the eastern sky. Each morning I would set my alarm and greet the sunrise. There was one morning we had a heavy frost and I had to bundle up really well, but it was worth it! As the sun rose, I imagined the bridegroom coming out of his chamber to greet me each day. The times spent on that deck were holy, intimate times with our Lord. I slept, prayed, and communed with my Lord through nature there. The view was breathtaking.

One particular day I was reading the Song of Songs and I felt the Lord wooing me as his words in scripture touched me deeply. It was a brisk spring evening as I re-read the verses.

My beloved speaks and says to me: "Arise, my love,
my fair one, and come away;
11 for lo, the winter is past, the rain is over and gone.
12 The flowers appear on the earth, the time of singing
has come, and the voice of the turtledove is heard
in our land.
13 The fig tree puts forth its figs, and the vines are in
blossom; they give forth fragrance. Arise, my love,
my fair one, and come away.
14 O my dove, in the clefts of the rock, in the covert of
the cliff, let me see your face, let me hear your voice,
for your voice is sweet, and your face is comely.
15 Catch us the foxes, the little foxes, that spoil the
vineyards, for our vineyards are in blossom.
16 My beloved is mine and I am his, he pastures his
flock among the lilies.
17 Until the day breathe and the shadows flee, turn,
my beloved, be like a gazelle, or a young stag upon rug-
ged mountains.

—Song of Solomon 2: 10-17.

As I read the lines I couldn't believe my ears. As I read about the turtle dove cooing in the land, I literally heard one singing nearby. My friend the dove sang for a while and as I listened, I cried. The Lord was so near I could almost feel him. If that wasn't enough a screech owl began her song. The deer had already shown their faces earlier. Maybe my winter was leaving and the new life of my springtime was coming.

Somehow I felt as though it didn't matter too much what was going on in my world anymore. My bridegroom was making his presence known to me. This is what I needed at this time. My prince had come and put his arm around me and everything was going to be OK! I felt peace and safety for the first time in a while. Could everything really work out for good? Romans 8:28 says so! We know that all things work together for good for those who love God, who are called according to his purpose.

MIDWAY THROUGH THE EIGHT DAYS, I had a break-through but it didn't come easy. The Lord awakened me in the middle of the night. It was around 3 a.m. on Friday morning. I clearly had a sense that the Holy Spirit wanted me to go into the chapel and pray. Remember I had spent a lot of time under the altar, so I had become quite comfortable in that chapel. It was a very short walk to the chapel from my room so I grabbed a blanket and a pillow and went quietly in obedience to be with the Lord.

When I got settled in, I felt a deep presence of the Lord with me. There was no light on in the chapel except that of the red sanctuary candle that sat before the tabernacle. Sitting beside Jesus in the tabernacle, there was perfect stillness and peace. Interiorly I heard the Lord tell me to prostrate myself on the floor in cruciform shape. Never questioning why, I got up and moved to the center isle of the chapel where I had more room; with my blanket and pillow in hand I did just that.

As I lay there with my arms outstretched, I began to cry again. One thing that I can say about how I felt was that God was BIG! His presence was BIG! He was POWERFUL! He was the great I AM. I felt a sensation of union and oneness. In that stillness and presence, I prayed prayers that I would call contemplative prayer. Not with words, but with intimacy and union. The peace of what I now know as my surrender to God, came over me.

It was a breaking of sorts that I experienced; yes life was hard at this point, and I was scared and didn't know what was next, but wasn't this somewhat how Jesus felt at times? Especially when he faced the cross. This was a pivotal point in the retreat when the many small ways that God had been dealing with me and leading me to this point climaxed.

I don't know how long I lay there awake, but the next thing I remember was Sr. Mary Catherine coming through the chapel to start breakfast. It was breaking dawn; but there was more breaking yet to come. God was not yet finished with my personal passion. More small deaths were to come during the daylight hours. It was actually really Friday, my Good Friday experience. I had fallen asleep in the arms of Jesus and really didn't fully understand what was happening until another day passed.

On this good Friday, my spiritual director gave me several Bible verses to read. The ones that seemed to really grab me were from the beatitudes. Yes, the Be-Attitudes. Slowly I read them and one by one I took them into my spirit. There was still that deep sense of presence of the Lord with me from my chapel experience during the night. Things were going fine until I got to the verse: ***"Blessed are those who are persecuted for righteousness' sake, for theirs is the kingdom of heaven.* - Matthew 5:10.**

As I pondered this verse, I began to cry. I thought the dam had already broke in the tear department, but there was still more cleansing that needed to take place. If you remember I stated earlier that I was angry at Kenny due to our financial situation. He didn't deserve this directed anger, but I had to put it on somebody. I also mentioned that I was angry at God and wasn't aware that

I was. At this point in my retreat, things got pretty rough. Little did I know that the screaming and yelling that I had joked about were soon to begin. I began to think about all the times that I felt persecuted for the sake of the kingdom of God and I began to get angrier.

Kenny, in our early years would "persecute" me during those years in our marriage when we were unequally yoked. I shared that in earlier chapters. Please know that he didn't intend to do me harm, we just didn't know how to handle the spiritual changes that we were undergoing as a couple. Has this happened with your spouse? Have you felt the sting of misunderstanding of your spirituality? If so, take time to bring this to the Lord.

It was time for my hour of direction with Marco and I was a wreck. My hair was wild, and I hadn't worn make-up for days. I looked like John the Baptist with swollen eyes. I told him about all the times I had been wounded by hurtful words. He listened so patiently and asked all the right questions.

My hour was up and as I stayed with this anger I felt that I had to get out and go for a walk. It was a beautiful day, so I set out after lunch. As I walked along the dirt road I got more angry. Blessed are those who can have a verse to be the ipecac medicine to induce expulsion of the interior poisons we hold on to. I began to think about what I had said on the first night of the retreat about screaming out loud. I sure had been doing a lot of yelling inwardly, so I thought maybe it's time to get this out. I looked for just the right spot to start yelling. There were houses along the road. They weren't too close together, yet they were close enough to the road that I thought that if I yelled too loud, someone might come and try to help me because they would think that I was in distress; or maybe they would think a crazy lady was on the loose! So I waited for the first place that I felt it was safe to yell.

At first, my yelling was a bit weak, but then I thought, who cares if someone hears me so I let it rip. It started to feel good so I yelled some more and then more deep heart sobbing came. As I yelled I realized I was angry at God too. Why did "*I* " have to carry this cross? Yes, I knew all the answers that were schooled in my religious brain, but I sure didn't like this cross. Not one bit. It was scary, and irksome and I didn't know what the outcome would be. I didn't like the feeling of total dependence on God for every single thing we consumed or needed. Would I have enough? Would we lose our house?

Matthew 6: 31–34 - *Therefore do not be anxious, saying, 'What shall we eat?' or 'What shall we drink?' or 'What shall we wear?'*

32 For the Gentiles seek all these things; and your heavenly Father knows that you need them all.

33 But seek first his kingdom and his righteousness, and all these things shall be yours as well.

34 "Therefore do not be anxious about tomorrow, for tomorrow will be anxious for itself. Let the day's own trouble be sufficient for the day."

Would I ever get it?

At this point I was starting to feel a release and I began to look around through the tears at the beauty of the countryside. I had walked a mile or so and began to notice pink plastic survey markers on this beautiful piece of property that was for sale. Not only did I notice the pink survey stakes, but I began to see these yellow signs of some sort nailed to some of the trees. One of the trees was a huge oak tree in the beautiful pasture I had been admiring. My curiosity was getting the best of me.

I knew how to cross a barbed wire fence, but considering I had been the crazy lady screaming a few minutes earlier, I decided it wasn't in my best interest to trespass so I kept walking. My senses were becoming keenly aware of my surroundings. What happened next was one of the biggest graces of my weekend. I noticed the same yellow sign on a cedar tree up ahead and it was right on the edge of the road. I couldn't wait to get close enough to read the yellow sign. As I read the small sign it said two simple words: "bearing tree" along with some legal descriptions of the property. I was overwhelmed as I read it. I had never seen a survey marker like this before. The thought kept running over and over in my mind, a bearing tree, a bearing tree. A bearing tree that was also a cedar tree. My mind and heart kept processing what I was seeing and feeling. I knew the Holy Spirit was speaking to me. I thought about scripture verses that referred to the cedars of Lebanon.

> *I will be as the dew to Israel; he shall blossom as the lily, he shall strike root as the poplar; 6 his shoots shall spread out; his beauty shall be like the olive, and his fragrance like Lebanon.*

> **—Hosea 14: 5-6.**

Cedars are fragrant and their aroma is often noticed from a distance. The smell was all part of the experience for me. It is said that cedars are a symbol of Christ and I've heard that the fragrance of a cedar is also associated as the aroma of Christ. So I stood there, gazing upon the bearing tree and my experience began to go even deeper. This is the fruit of silence.

The surveyor had cut three gashes in the tree. This bearing tree had become a symbol of the cross and of Jesus to me. One gash was where the head would be, one near the heart area and the last one near the feet. The gashes were oozing the sap from where it had been cut. Not only did the sign speak volumes to me, but the surveyor's gashes had become the symbol of the wounds of Christ and his precious blood He had given for me!

As I stood there looking at the bearing tree, I heard The Holy Spirit speak to my soul. "I am your bearing tree. My child, there have been days that you carried your burden all alone. I am your burden bearer. I am your bearing tree. I will bear your burdens but I also am your boundary marker. I will keep you pointed to true north. If you stay within my boundaries, you will not get lost again amid the pain. Will you not let me help you? Surrender this to me and you will find peace. This is your 'good Friday.' This is where you must surrender your agenda and crucify it on the cross. When you learn to accept this cross that you have been carrying, it becomes less burdensome. Yes , I called you into the chapel last night. That was your agony in the garden, but today is 'Good Friday' and in your Surrender you will soon find your resurrection."

The revelation that I received on that walk is embedded into my heart forever. A flood of peace and awe fell over me. I was broken yet again to be made more in the image of my Lord. My walk back was swifter now with a sense of purpose and resolve. By the grace of God I did leave the stress and worry at the foot of the bearing tree. I made a little altar on the side of the road with some rocks I found and I placed some wildflowers on the altar. It was my place of sacrifice and remembering. That little rock altar represented my sacred encounter with the living God. I also knew full well that Jesus was my sacrificial lamb and the he had offered himself on the altar for me. Surely I could unite my sacrifice with his and it could become something beautiful!

Colossians 1:24 - *Now I rejoice in what I am suffering for you, and I fill up in my flesh what is still lacking in regard to Christ's afflictions, for the sake of his body, which is the church.*

ON ANOTHER NOTE, not all days while on retreat are so deep; but there is always a deep intimacy between you and the Lord. My heart will always be tender as I share these next experiences. It is now about five years later and I am on my way to spend another eight days in silence. I chose St. Mary's By the Sea at Cape May, New Jersey. It is an unbelievable place run by the Sisters of St. Joseph. While on this retreat, I experienced a deeper awareness of God's love for me, refreshment, a conviction and delight, to name a few things.

The retreat center was right on the Atlantic Ocean, so I had time to stroll the beach each day. I got into a rhythm of prayer, food, rest, swim, prayer, food, rest and swim. It was a beautiful sacred space to rejuvenate my body, soul and spirit. This particular year, my body was pretty beat up. I had a surgery on my knee after battling with pain for a long period of time and it had taken its toll on me in many ways.

My retreat director was a professed religious woman in the order of the St. Joseph sisters. The Holy Spirit did a great job matching us up. I really needed to rest and heal my body as much as anything and she could sense this, so she told me on the first day to just stroll and take in the beauty of God in my surroundings. There would be no recommended scripture verses for today, so off I went to explore. I was like a kid in the candy shop. I can see and experience God very easily in nature.

I love the beach, so I immediately put on my bathing suit and headed for the shoreline. The beach at Cape May has lots of small pebbles in the sand. The array of colors of the rocks was mesmerizing. The amount of small stones on the shoreline was immense. As I was walking along looking for that special rock and shell, I was pondering how much God loves me and had even asked Him to reveal this to me in a tangible way.

Before the retreat, the Lord had told me he was going to show me his indwelling presence within me and how much He loved me. While walking and praying with these thoughts in mind, my eyes zeroed in on a particular rock. It sat among thousands of small pebbles, but there it was: a perfect shaped heart. No imagination was needed to see this. I picked it up with great delight as if I had just found a ten-carat diamond. It was such a precious find to reinforce what the Holy Spirit was telling me. I tucked it away for safe keeping.

Several hours passed by and I was walking the beach again. I love to find treasures of any kind. As I was looking down, I couldn't believe what I saw; there was another heart rock. Tears welled up in my eyes as I pondered how much the Lord was trying to tell me that he loved me. I held the rock to my heart and savored the experience. Now, I can be a bit persistent with the Lord. I did believe he loved me but as I walked I asked the Lord for a small favor. The conversation went something like this: "Lord I know that you love me, and I love my two very special rocks. You have given me one for the Father's love, one for the Son's love, could I be so bold as to ask for one more for the Holy Spirit's love?" To my delight, I looked down and there was the third one. Each rock had a unique shape that spoke to me in wonderful ways. I've included a picture of them for you to enjoy. He's crazy about you! You're His favorite kid!

Here is what I journaled after finding the rocks.

THE THREE ROCKS

It wasn't written down in word nor spoken to me by another,
Yeah I found thee by the shore.
If I had looked for you in the book or listened to music on this
day- I would have missed your trinitarian heart.
At first there was one, and I was given great delight
and then there were two and it was such a great sight!
Should I keep on looking for more of you?
There's never an end. . .
And there it was my triple delight - Some see rocks,
I see love.
Love from the one who called me by name and walks with me
hand-in-hand on the shore
Open your eyes and your heart, you say to me
look around and feel my majesty!
There are seasons to work and seasons to rest and to play;
give yourself permission to be able to do both
Yes, I come to you and walk with you on the seashore
Take great delight in me because there's always more.
The heart rocks grew each time you found one;
Your love for me will do just the same
For every day spent with me is never in vain.
You may feel my presence in varying degrees
But, my child, I am with you through joy and in pain.
Humble yourself before me each day and I will lead you and
guide you every step of the way.
Some see rocks, you see love; gifts from me sent from heaven
above.
A new day has dawned and you will surely see my glory and
splendor and your great dignity.
I want you to know that I dwell within you
Tis a truth you have known but I will reveal ever new.

> Rest now, my bride, refresh and renew
> This time now is spent just me and you.
> Yes, some see rocks, but you see love, sent from your creator
> made with great love!

What do the images of the rocks speak to you? One lesson is to not always expect the same thing. This trip was about the rocks or was it? God will do anything to speak to you. Are you listening? The Lord told me he was doing something new. Instead of shells this teaching was about the rocks; but that didn't stop me from searching for the perfect shell. So I will share another story.

A few days had passed since my arrival and each day had the same rhythm. I had gotten up early to beach comb. There were huge rock jetties every so many feet to stop erosion. I was talking to the Lord and thinking if I were a shell, I'd probably be hanging around those big rocks. You know, it's where you get off course a bit and then you're stranded in a tight place. It only made sense that there could be some pretty nice shells between those big rocks; so each day I looked.

As I was searching, I saw something beneath the surface of the sand. The waves were coming in and out so it was hard to keep an eye on what looked like a big shell. It was quite large and I noticed that the shell had a royal blue color to it as well as tones of pink and creme. I couldn't tell how big it was because of it being buried, so I began digging around it. I would get lots of the sand away and the water would wash the sand back over it. This beautiful shell was wedged between two very large rocks. I couldn't believe what I had found. I had never seen a shell like this on the Florida panhandle; I was on the Atlantic! It was some type of conch or whelk shell. I pulled and dug and prayed, but I just couldn't get it out. After trying for about 30 minutes, I felt like the Lord said, it's not for you. The shell was for me to admire. I am persistent; I thought to myself: "maybe later, maybe tomorrow." I would look again at a lower tide.

With a full tummy, my Bible, journal, chair and towel I went for my afternoon siesta and walk on the beach. I decided to take my walk as soon as I claimed my spot on the sand. As I walked along the shoreline, I saw two teenage girls approaching me and they were giggling with delight. I was green with envy when I saw that they had about six big beautiful whelk shells in their arms.

The temptation to talk overcame me. There were no silence police on my retreat so I stopped them and said: "Girls, God sure has blessed you! Where did you find all those shells?" They were so excited they could barely talk. "We found them in the rock jetties." I told them about my find earlier and they said let us help you get it out. I explained to them that I really shouldn't be talking and why I wasn't supposed to be talking, but they were intrigued as we walked. "Are you a Christian?" they asked me. I told them I sure was. Guess what? One rock jetty looks just like the other and I couldn't find "my" shell. I thanked them for trying and, as I was coveting their shells, this was what was going on in my head. "OK Lord, they have more shells than I think they need. Why don't you tell them to give me one. I sure would like one of those!" The next thing I knew, one of the girls asked me if I wanted one of their shells! I was dumbfounded. I said: "If you're sure, of course, I would love one!"

All the shells were perfect except for one. It had a hole in it and of course that's the one she gave me. I sat there with a full heart, thanking God for my shell for I was truly grateful, and suddenly my heart went from gratefulness to spoiled rotten!

The Lord quickly began to give me an earful. He first asked me if I would have given up any of my shells if it had been the other way around. If I am honest here, I more than likely wouldn't have. The reason is because I think we all have times when we think of God as a God of scarcity instead of a God of abundance. The Holy Spirit was quickening me of something that I needed to confess. How many times did the Lord give me something and I didn't think it was enough, good enough, or I wanted something better. He took me through different times in my life that I wasn't satisfied with what he had provided. It was like scenes from a movie with me as the star of the show.

Doesn't this have a familiar story line here? I was just like the Jews! God provided hoar frost every day for them but it wasn't good enough. The Jews grumbled about everything! *And the people spoke against God and against Moses, "Why have you brought us up out of Egypt to die in the wilderness? For there is no food and no water, and we loathe this worthless food." Numbers 21:5*

I tell you, I was a bit ashamed of myself. Here I was grumbling with my mouth full. The Lord doesn't always give you what you want, but he always gives you what you need! This cracked shell caused me to fall on my face in repentance for so many places I hadn't been grateful.

The shell just kept on giving. In direction the next day, I discovered how I put myself in an expectancy of perfection so many times. I was telling her how I had the teaching from the Lord the day before. I also had shared with her that the priest I went to confession with told me that I had a beautiful light that beamed out of me. I say this with great humility. As I was speaking to my director, she asked me if people are drawn to perfect people. I said, in my opinion, not usually. People who tend to be perfect are not easy to be around. The people that I like to be around are the ones who have experienced brokenness.

My director then said: "Debbie, let me see your shell." As soon as I held it up, I knew where this was going. She then said: "If we are vessels that hold the living God, how can our Lord's light be seen in us if we are perfect and don't have a few cracks like this shell? The light within you, Debbie, has to shine through your cracks."

I wept in the goodness of the Lord during this hour of Spiritual Direction. I want to add that the next day I saw a man digging in the jetties. Yes, you guessed it. He had found my beautiful shell. I had to go see for sure. It was my shell alright. I explained to him that I actually had found it but couldn't pull it out. In honesty, I still wanted that shell, even though the Lord said it wasn't mine the day before. I watched him tug and pull until he was able to remove it. He was so excited to bring it to his wife. He told me he had come to this place for years and had never found anything so beautiful. As he walked away, it brought me joy to see him with his treasure from the sea. There are just some things, even though they are so beautiful, that the Lord says: "Not this time, Debbie. I will bless you with the things that I want you to have. There will always be others who have something that you desire; learn contentment."

On another day at Cape May, I was praying with the scripture from **Isaiah 64:8 -** *Yet, O Lord, thou art our Father; we are the clay, and thou art our potter; we are all the work of thy hand.*

As I sat with this verse, I envisioned myself on the potter's wheel. As I sat there, I said: "Lord, what type of pottery piece am I? Am I a tall vase, or a pitcher? What do I look like to you?"

As I waited I felt that the Lord spoke and He said: "You are a basin. You are wide and deep and you hold water that refreshes others. You are a vessel of service. My children can come and be refreshed with **MY** living water that you contain. Yes, you are a basin that contains rivers of living water. Will you let me use you?"

This image is one that I hold very dear to my heart. I wanted to find a piece of pottery that would remind me of this image so I kept my eyes open, but nothing came. It was almost a year later when to my surprise, my sweet husband said one morning that he wanted to take me on a leisurely drive. This is something we both love to do. Arkansas is a beautiful state with a primitive beauty that still has areas of simplicity that are unspoiled.

Kenny had a specific route in mind. We would travel to the Ozarks to an area near the Buffalo River called Osage. The reason he wanted to go there was that we had both seen a special on a local television station about an old general store that a potter owned. I really had forgotten about my basin at this point. . . or at least the quest to find one.

As I walked into the old storefront, I thought; Lord you are up to something here aren't you? The store was called the Stamps General Store and it was built in 1901. It had a variety of original items that dated back to the early 1900s. My heart raced a bit when I saw the potter working at the wheel. ***So I went down to the potter's house, and there he was working at his wheel* - Jeremiah 18:3.**

I imagined that Papa was shaping me on the wheel.

I knew that Papa wanted me to get the fullness of my experience a year earlier at Cape May. He wanted me to find my basin here. I told the potter my story and asked him if he had such an item already made. He just kept working and told me to look around. He said that he had made a pitcher and basin for a minister, and then he just kept working. I believe he wanted me to seek out the piece that God wanted me to have without the potter's opinion. It was fascinating to watch him work.

Besides all the artifacts, he had many beautiful pieces of pottery for sale. I circled the store over and over again looking for just the right piece. I just wasn't seeing what I wanted and was resolved that I might not find it when I laid my eyes on what I thought was MY basin. It was in an obscure place away from the bulk of his pieces. As I gazed upon it, I knew it was just right. Maybe it wasn't a true basin , but the piece spoke to my heart. The inside was a beautiful shade of blue, like what living water would represent, The outer part of the basin was brown; of the earth, like me. Jesus was the blue on the inside and I was the brown on the outside. Not only was the piece brown on the outside, It had lines drawn on it, that to me, represented that life leaves us a bit marred at times. It also had some places where the paint had dripped, just another symbol to me that I have imperfections just like the basin. I realized as I purchased the piece, that God had given me a chance and a way to always savor and remember that sacred moment on my silent retreat. When we have an encounter with God, it lasts for a lifetime. We can go back to those moments and draw from the graces again and again.

I HAVE ONE MORE AWESOME STORY I want to share from when I was at Cape May. On the first night of an eight-day retreat you get an orientation. Each person who has a role in the retreat explains the part they play. Toward the end of orientation a lady stood up and said: "I am the masseuse here. If you would like a massage while here, there is a sign-up sheet in the foyer." I was a bit surprised because I had never been on a retreat where there was a massage therapist.

I thought to myself; this is pretty cool, maybe I should get a massage while here, but I quickly convinced myself that it was too frivolous for me to do that. I argued back and forth with myself for days about this. Each day I would go by the sign-up sheet for a massage and each day I would say to myself that I should be grateful that I got to come and be content. Finally around day four I said what the heck, I'm going to sign up for a massage on the last full day of the retreat. What's another $60? I thought to myself, you won't do without food because you're getting a massage, but I also thought that if I decided to back out, scheduling the massage on the last day would give me time to do so.

It was Sunday and the day for my massage had come. I did my usual routine and went to the beach after lunch. I set my alarm on my phone in case I fell asleep. I was still feeling guilty for spending the money on myself when the alarm went off on my phone. What happened next made me cry and then I broke out in laughter. At the same time my alarm was going off on my phone to remind me it was time for my massage, an airplane was flying over me. If you've been to the beach you will know what I'm talking about when I tell you that it was a plane that flew by each day with a big banner flowing behind it advertising something. I had seen the planes all week but not once did I see this advertisement! I was gathering my chair and towel when I looked up and the banner said: "You deserve a massage today!" I cried and laughed and I said to the Lord: " OK, OK, I am going to get the massage. I hear you."

I then heard His reply back to me: " I don't know why you're worrying about the money, I'm the one paying for it." If you recall, I told you earlier about how my body was beaten up from work and wrestling with a bad knee. Our Lord wanted to give me the touch of healing through the gifted hands of the masseuse. The massage felt so wonderful that I cried. After receiving the massage, the pain in my hip that I was having from the injury in my knee was gone. Once again I was blessed and pleasantly surprised as the Lord ministered to me. God is very personal and he does speak to us. We just have to make time to listen and look for him.

Many times the Lord begins to speak prior to a deep experience. I was anticipating going to Grand Coteau, Louisiana, for eight days of silence. Let me just say that this is a wonderful retreat center run by the Jesuits. Imagine yourself on beautiful manicured acreage, sitting under massive Live Oak trees that are hundreds of years old. Azaleas are blooming in a cemetery that dates back to the Civil War era. Wonderful meals are cooked for you three times daily and you are in a newly renovated facility that helps you experience total comfort.

Prior to attending the retreat, when I would enter into prayer, I would see myself with a bald head. This happened for about a month prior to going. This is when I became aware that God was wanting to say something to me, but I wasn't sure or I just didn't pray through it long enough. I didn't get a feeling that I was being shown anything that was bad. I told Kenny and knowing that I try to be obedient, his reply to me telling him about seeing myself with a bald head was: "You better not come back with a shaved head!" I assured him that wouldn't happen.

This retreat was also the same one that I started getting to know my mother Mary better. Well, back to my experience.

As I mentioned before, sometimes you get a purging in the silent days while you are meditating. On this particular day, I could see that the Lord was dealing with me in the area of my pride. He began to show me areas that he wanted me to own up to and go to confession. For those of you reading this, it's quite humbling to go to another human being and admit those areas that are not Christlike; but after reconciliation, there's no better feeling of freedom and mercy.

So I am wrestling with this pride issue. I'm talking battling flesh and spirit head-on. I had found my favorite evening spot on the west side of the second floor balcony. I really never saw anyone else there so it was a great place to read, ruminate, and watch the beauty of the sunsets. I was given several verses that day and I honestly don't remember if the Holy Spirit led me to this particular verse or if I was assigned it, but it was from *Mark 1: 40-45* and as I read it I became wide-eyed.

And a leper came to him beseeching him, and kneeling said to him, "If you will, you can make me clean."
41 Moved with pity, he stretched out his hand and touched him, and said to him, "I will; be clean."
42 And immediately the leprosy left him, and he was made clean.
43 And he sternly charged him, and sent him away at once,
44 and said to him, "See that you say nothing to any one; but go, show yourself to the priest, and offer for your cleansing what Moses commanded, for a proof to the people."
45 But he went out and began to talk freely about it, and to spread the news, so that Jesus could no longer openly enter a town, but was out in the country; and people came to him from every quarter.

Yes, I was a leper. I had the disease of pride and I needed cleansing. I knew I must make a good confession the next morning, but I was having such a hard time admitting my areas of pridefulness.

The struggle was real. As I read the scripture over and over, something new jumped out at me. After Jesus cleansed him, he told him to go show himself to the priest. Now I was going to show myself to the priest, but what did the priest do in the old testament after the cleansing? The Holy Spirit directed me to Leviticus where the laws and customs were written. As I poured through the chapter headings there it was; Leviticus 14, Law of cleansing a leper. The priest in those days did a ritual cleansing and after he pronounced him clean, the cleansed leper was to shave his head. *14:9 and on the seventh day he shall shave all his hair off his head; he shall shave off his beard and his eyebrows, all his hair. Then he shall wash his clothes, and bathe his body in water, and he shall be clean.*

I was awestruck as I read this. Now, I knew I must go to the priest in the morning. God was speaking weeks before so that, at that moment, I would know for sure that the Lord was speaking to me. I would recognize the image he had given me. The bearing of my head metaphorically was my face-to-face confession. I would be laid bare and made clean through the sacrament of reconciliation. Morning couldn't come soon enough! I confessed and wept right then and there for my sins, but I needed to hear that priest say:" You're sins have been forgiven." So the next morning I heard the priest say these very words. Jesus had cleansed me!

While these experiences that I've shared might seem foreign to you, they happened and they happened because I was waiting and listening for the Lord. I was silent before him. Had I attended an eight-day retreat in my earlier years, I might not have gotten anything like the experiences I shared. You don't have to be a deep spiritual person to hear God speak. You do have to make time for him! What I want you to take away from this chapter is that God is as near as your breath each and every day. We have to have times of silence in our lives whether it's ten minutes a day (which is always needed) or one day or eight days. If we're always talking and doing, we aren't really listening are we?

If you desire a greater intimacy with the Lord, why don't you just stop for a moment and take time to just get still before the Lord? Ask Him to give you the grace of hearing Him and greater intimacy. He is waiting for you.

⇒✝⇐

CHAPTER 8
POWER OF PRAYER

I've talked about prayer and the types of prayer and, I suppose, there could be myriads of prayers or ways of praying, as many as the grains of sand on the seashore. This chapter is not about how to pray but about answered prayer. As you read, I want you to see the goodness of God and I hope that the words on these pages will stoke up a fire within you to pray. I ask the Lord to move your heart to amazement, tears, and desire as I share just a few of the prayer experiences I've had. Some have been mentioned already, but I have a few more that I want to share. With each experience I have grown in a specific area. Now, where do I start?

As I tell this first story, this is from my perspective and my experience. I am certain that if you were to ask my son and his wife, they would have a different perspective of what they experienced on this journey since it was happening to them; but as it happened to them, it happened to all of our family. Twenty-one years ago my oldest son married the love of his life. Trey and Laura were married for a few years when we learned that Laura needed exploratory surgery. She was experiencing severe pain and the doctor suspected female issues. Family came to the hospital that day to be with them. Prior to the surgery, it was all just hypothetical theories of what could be going on. Before the surgery, I remember Laura feeling anxiety about what could or would happen. As I think back, it was a very frightening time for my 21-year-old daughter-in-law. One of the things that I recall was her worry before being put to sleep that she would wake up and her ovaries would be gone. I specifically remember telling her that this would never happen. The doctor wouldn't just remove her ovaries without her permission.

Time came for her surgery and they wheeled her away. We all waited anxiously in the waiting room. As we waited and wondered the what ifs, the doctor called from the operating room for my son. When he got off the phone with the doctor, he explained to us that one of Laura's ovaries had ruptured and that he needed Trey's permission to remove it. I remember him saying that the ovary was so disfigured that it looked like hamburger meat and it was unrecognizable as an ovary. I couldn't believe what I was hearing. As I recall the scenes unfolding the day of the surgery, I can still remember how I felt as the doctor came out and spoke to us after the surgery.

The doctor kept shaking his head. He kept saying, "I'm so sorry." He told us Laura's abdomen was full of blood from the rupture. He said he didn't know how she had stood the pain. The next words that came out of his mouth numbed me. He said: "I'm sorry to tell you that I don't think she will ever be able to have children." She had a pretty bad case of endometriosis and not only did she lose the one ovary, but her other ovary was diseased and had cysts on it. When those words came off his lips, what I heard was "your son just died." He didn't say that, but that's how it felt.

The deepest sorrow and pain came over me. I felt that I might faint. In a matter of a few seconds, it felt as if the course of my life had just changed and I was preparing for a funeral. In some way, I guess I was. Being told that my son and his wife might not have a child, and that I might not have a grandchild hurt me deeply. I can only imagine what Trey was feeling. I felt as if I had lost something very precious. I felt hopeless. Thank you, Lord, that I didn't get stuck in that place! The Lord began to speak to me in signs and wonders and His word.

At this particular time in my life, I was learning about the power of the tongue and the fact that we can either speak life or death.

> **Death and life are in the power of the tongue,
> and those who love it will eat its fruits.**

> **—Proverbs 18:21**

Another way I've seen this paraphrased is: "Every word spoken becomes a positive living thing to either minister or destroy."

Just stop here for a minute and think about what's coming out of your mouth. "I am so stupid, I can't change, I am always sick." Why not think and say: "Thank you, Lord, that I have the mind of Christ, thank you that your grace is sufficient to help me change, Thank you, Lord, that by your stripes I am healed. Thank you, Lord, that what you call me to do I will be successful in it"?

> **But he was wounded for our transgressions, he
> was bruised for our iniquities; upon him was the
> chastisement that made us whole, and with his stripes
> we are healed.**

> **—Isaiah 53:5**

By the grace of God, He began to quicken my spirit to speak positive words of hope and healing. Dr. Jesus can do anything!

At this same time in my life, I was also going through a tough time as we struggled to keep my mother at home with caregivers for her dementia. At this point, she had been struggling with this disease for nearly 14 years. Even though my four siblings and I didn't all see eye-to-eye, the time came when we had to place my mother in a nursing home. I bring this up now because the day we moved her, I was enroute to Little Rock with so much going on in my mind that the next thing I knew, I was being pulled over for speeding. The officer really didn't seem to care as I told him what I was dealing with. He wrote the ticket and told me where I could pay the fine. I cried all the way to my destination with great sorrow in my heart.

As the story of infertility unfolded, this speeding ticket was a grace because sometime later when I went to pay the ticket, it was the same day that my daughter-in-law was having her surgery. I went to pay the fine after the surgery and right on the counter where I was paying was a scripture verse that became my strength as we dealt with the infertility and my mother.

Fear not, for I am with you, be not dismayed, for I am your God; I will strengthen you, I will help you, I will uphold you with my victorious right hand.

—Isaiah 41:10

These words were like a balm to my frightened soul. I had a lot of fear raging in me. Would Trey and Laura have children? Would my family make it through the transition of my mother being moved from her home? Would we be strong enough to endure what was coming? I kept hearing the words "fear not" in my inner being.

WHAT IS FRIGHTENING YOU right now? What fear has a hold on you now? Quit listening to the enemy and his lies! The enemy starts putting these thoughts of fear and doom in our minds and before we know it, they have consumed us. No matter what you're facing right now, God is with you and upholding you! This verse became a mantra for me. When I was having a fearful day, that verse would show up in front of me! God will use any means that he can to reach us if we are in tune to his voice and ways.

As the months rolled by, we kept getting difficult reports on the possibility of a grandchild. By the grace of God, my faith was unwavering most of the time. I don't think I have ever experienced such faith since then. We kept getting negative reports; but I would confess to everyone, especially Trey and Laura, that no matter what anyone said, I knew in every inch of my being that they were going to have a baby.

This wasn't just positive thinking from a human perspective, it was divinely placed within me! I didn't know how or when they would become pregnant, but I was willing to keep the faith, pray and wait. I'll never forget one such day that I was being tested to keep believing. I also had held onto the fact that Abraham and Sarah conceived in what seemed like an impossible situation. I was at work, it was late in the day, and I was cutting Trey's hair. He was giving me the latest fertility report and frankly it didn't sound good to me; when in walked a woman I had never seen before.

This woman looked like she might have been of Pentecostal faith by the way she was dressed and the way she wore her hair. She was selling homemade music cassettes. She seemed kind and, even though I didn't want to buy one, I felt compelled to help her with her financial needs. She thanked me for my kindness and left. Just a few minutes had passed and she came back in the salon. She told me that the Lord had sent her back in and wanted to know if I had a prayer request. I told her that this was my son sitting in my chair and I told her of our desire for he and Laura to have a baby. She began praying and calling into being that which was not yet seen. She prayed many words, but she looked me square in the eye and said two specific things that made me know without a shadow of doubt that God had sent her in to us at a low time. She recounted the story of Abraham and Sarah overcoming impossible situations to have Isaac and then she quoted, you guessed it, **Isaiah 41:10**

- fear not, for I am with you, be not dismayed, for I am your God, I will strengthen you, I will help you, I will uphold you with my victorious right hand.

I knew the presence of God was with us and that God was working in all of our lives. As I played the cassette that I bought from her, I didn't think it was very good musically, but the words I heard penetrated my heart. The words being sung said: stay the knife Abraham, you will not have to offer your son, I will provide. My faith thermometer went sky high! I believe you can do anything Lord! It was as if that day in the hospital where I felt I had lost all my dreams had vanished. My son would live on after all through his child. God promised that Abraham's offspring would be as numerous as the stars in the sky and that his descendants would be a blessing! I claimed this verse as well. *I will make your descendants as numerous as the stars in the sky and will give them all these lands, and through your offspring all nations on earth will be blessed,* **- Genesis 26:4**

MONTHS TURNED INTO A YEAR or more and we still had no indication that our prayers were being heard, but we held the line. While we waited, Kenny and I began to do novenas. A novena is a nine-day rote prayer for a specific intention. We prayed with many different saints and even called upon the help of family members in heaven.

One particular saint that I am personally fond of is St. Therese the Little Flower. Her feast day is on my birthday, so you can see why I am fond of her. We began a novena to her in the fall of 1999 and finished it right before All Saints Day. Kenny and I were in St. Louis for a regional Cursillo meeting and, upon touring the city, we were excited to see that St. Theresa's relics were in the city. I had a gentle nudge that she was saying, "I am praying with you."

Our final destination was Our Lady of the Snows in Belleville, Illinois. Many people had gathered there for the regional meeting. There was quite a stir going on among the attendees. One lady came up to me and asked if I had been in the main church. People were overwhelmed at the display of roses in the sanctuary. I had to see what all the fuss was about. When I entered the church I began to cry. There were over 60,000 roses arrayed everywhere! Each one represented a loved one in lieu of a $1.00 donation. As I gazed at all of the beauty with tear-filled eyes, I knew St Theresa was giving me the promised sign of roses after completing the novenas. It was overwhelming! My spirit was as high as a kite once again.

It is now Mother's day in the year 2000. I was in a bit of a low place as we had not yet gotten the news of an upcoming pregnancy. At Mass that morning I begged Mother Mary, my mama Rose and any other saint, especially St. Therese, to please see if there wasn't something they could do about this situation. Our family all gathered together at Trey and Laura's house. My husband brought the mothers in the family a corsage or a rose (I don't remember which it was) and he even included Laura. I wasn't sure if this was a good idea but Kenny handed it to her and said you might be a mother right now and not even know it. We got it in our heads that might even be the reason they had invited us to their house this particular time. We left with heavy hearts because we didn't get the news. I remember crying all the way home and feeling like giving her the flowers might have been like pouring salt into a wound. Had he done the right thing? Sometimes you just don't know, but you have to release the faith and act upon it.

I kept calling into being that which was not yet seen. *Romans 4:17 says: as it is written, "I have made you the father of many nations"—in the presence of the God in whom he believed, who gives life to the dead and calls into existence the things that do not exist.* Guess what? Six days later, we got the phone call! I can still hear those words to this day: "Mom, you're going to be a grandma!" Laura was actually pregnant on Mother's Day. We just did not know it yet!

There's one more thing I must add before I close this story. We were on our way to a softball tournament for our youngest daughter when we got the call. I was on cloud nine and had my head in the clouds. When we got to the bleachers, I realized I had left my sunglasses in the car and I went back out to get them. Stay with me now. My mother's name was Rose and at her funeral we played Bette Midler's song "The Rose." As I approached my car I could hear the song "The Rose" blaring on someone's car stereo. That song wasn't even very popular at this time. As I looked around for my sunglasses, I reached under the seat to get them and I felt some paper. As I pulled the paper out, I was in awe because it was the photographs from Our Lady of the Snow's sanctuary with all the roses. One week earlier I was begging my mama and St. Therese to intercede and today they were telling me they did. What a mighty God we serve! Our precious granddaughter and her sister are now 17 and 15 years old. When man says you can't, God says I can!

My next story has so many facets to it, but I'm going to concentrate on one very special part. Kenny, my dear friend Diane and I were heading home from a healing retreat in southern Louisiana. We had spent about 48 hours in praise, prayer and teaching with Maria Vadia, an author and speaker active in the Catholic charismatic movement. I have been to many retreats and conferences but this one was very special. The three of us had each received many graces and gifts during that time we spent with the Lord. We left and we were on fire! We felt so full of fresh fire that I honestly thought we might be glowing. You know, like Moses looked when he came down off the mountain. He had the shekinah glory all over him.

Shekinah comes from the Hebrew word "shekinot" and describes where God is dwelling, settling or where His Divine Presence is. Shekinah is seen when God's glory filled the Temple and when the Israelites wandered in the wilderness and He was a light during the night.

(Read more at http://www.patheos.com/blogs/christiancrier/2014/05/17/what-is-shekinah-glory-is-this-in-the-bible/#6vzLrhM6c43qf7yR.99)

Our hearts were full as we set out for our eight-hour drive back home. God uses everything and orchestrates our every move to accomplish His will. Because the retreat center was in the deep south, it had satsuma trees on the grounds. The fruit was ripening and we were told to help ourselves to what we wanted of it. We had never seen this particular fruit before. It is of importance to mention this fruit because on our way back home, we saw a fruit stand on the side of the road selling it. Diane said: "Oh look, there's satsuma for sale." Kenny asked us if we wanted him to stop for some, and we said sure. I should have known God was up to something, because we NEVER stop on long drives except for the restroom! You could say that was the first sign that something special had happened, especially since we were only about 15-20 minutes down the road. We got out and purchased our fruit and we were on our way back home.

Let me just say that I love everything about Louisiana; the food, the faith, the people, and their culture. I was disappointed that we didn't get to eat any blue crabs while there. We had only traveled another 15 minutes or so and I started seeing signs for live blue crabs for sale. I mentioned it a few times thinking that Kenny would never stop again since we had such a long drive ahead of us. Kenny said: "Do you want me to stop again?" Delighted with his question I said:" Oh, would you? Yes, please stop." We pulled over and I went in the primitive roadside fish market. There was a big, burly man behind the counter with a woman in the back, standing by the sink, picking the meat from the crabs.

I had two needs that I was hoping he could help me with. I asked him if he had any crabs for sale and, if so, did he have a cheap Styrofoam cooler I could purchase to transport them in? My heart jumped for joy when he said "yes" on both counts! I had him get me two dozen from the holding tank and I went inside to pay. This was also an educational trip for Diane since she had never seen live crabs before. She had gotten out to see the tank of them and Kenny and Diane then went back into the vehicle to wait for me.

As best I can remember, the price for the crabs was about $24. I told the man all I had was a $100 bill and two twenties. He didn't take credit cards and he didn't have any change. He told me to just give him $20 and we'd call it even. I felt bad in shorting him because I know how hard these people work for their money, but he insisted, so I gave him the $20, but asked him his name because I would say some prayers for him in return for the balance.

He handed me his business card with his name and phone number on it but instead of praying for him, he asked me to pray for the lady by the sink picking crabs. This made me so happy because I love to pray with people and I knew I was so full of fresh fire from the Holy Spirit, something good had to happen. I asked him what was she needing prayers for and he said she was full of cancer. I looked at her and asked if she was open to being prayed over and she said yes. Excusing myself, I told them that I was going out to the car for some more "fresh fire" reinforcements. I told Kenny and Diane they had to come back inside because we had an assignment from God. They never hesitated a bit, didn't ask a question, but obediently followed me inside. I explained what was going on as we hurried back in the store.

There were a couple of booths where people could sit, so we asked the woman to sit in the booth as we surrounded her. The three of us and the man stood round her as I explained to her where we had been and about how God is still in the business of healing. I believe that before you pray over people you should explain to them what you are going to do and then make sure that they want prayer. There are times when I pray over people that I will use my Charismatic prayer language and at other times I don't. This was one time that I knew I should, so I explained to her that she would hear us praying in a strange language and we would use blessed oil. As I continued, I explained that we would operate in the charismatic gifts and pray for healing.

> *Is any among you sick? Let him call for the elders of the church, and let them pray over him, anointing him with oil in the name of the Lord; 15 and the prayer of faith will save the sick man, and the Lord will raise him up; and if he has committed sins, he will be forgiven. 16 Therefore confess your sins to one another, and pray for one another, that you may be healed. The prayer of a righteous man has great power in its effects.*

—James 5:14-16.

After saying this verse to her I asked her if she still wanted prayer and her reply will remain with me forever. She said: **"I have been waiting for you!"** I could hardly believe what she said and I will talk about that it in a bit. She told us her condition was very serious, and that she was going to the doctor in a few days to determine the next course of action because she was pretty much at the end of her treatment options, and her cancer kept progressing.

We all prayed and I anointed her with the blessed oil. She was shedding tears and so was the burly fisherman. Somehow, I knew God was doing a powerful work. We all hugged her after praying, they thanked us and we went on our way. When we got back in the car, we all looked at each other and wondered what just had happened. We knew that we were on an assignment from God.

Now here's where I want to throw in a bit of teaching experience that I've learned over the years. We weren't but a few minutes down the road and I started thinking about all the things I should have prayed, or should have said. When God has worked through you, the enemy will come to cause you to feel like you missed the mark or to make you doubt. Don't listen to the enemy! We had been obedient and it didn't matter what we had said, God was the one doing the work. We were just His vessels. As we shared our perspective in the car for the next few minutes, I remembered I had the man's business card. I put the phone number in my phone under the name "crab lady" and thought that I would text them later with all the things I wanted to still tell them. For whatever reason, I never did text them and I'm glad I didn't because God was going to do some more faith work in me and it wouldn't have been as powerful if I had texted them right after.

Several years later, Kenny and I were watching a television show about the swamps of Louisiana. It was a Sunday afternoon and the show reminded me of the "crab lady." I looked over to Kenny and I said, "I wonder how the crab lady is doing." At first he didn't know who I was talking about and then he said: "Why don't you call her and see?"

My first reaction was that I didn't have her phone number to call her. My second thought was that she probably had died. I didn't want to know if she had because it would feel like our wonderful prayer experience at the roadside fish market would be only a pleasant memory. That was the enemy trying to cause doubt and to block the grace that was about to come to us.

As I sat there and savored that day some years earlier, I remembered that I actually did have her phone number. Remember, I was going to text her with all the things I should have said. Do you see what you just read? The things that *I* would have said. . . It's not our words, but Jesus that does the healing! I began to pray that the Holy Spirit would remind me how I had listed the phone number, and as I prayed the Holy Spirit recalled to my mind that it was under "crab lady." I got a few butterflies in my tummy and knew I had to have the courage to make the call. No matter what the outcome was, God had manifested His glory that day and it was up to him to bring the results. I went to the "C's" and there was her phone number. As I punched the number in, I was praying about what I would say. Would I get an answer? Would she be alive? Would they even remember us? Was this still their phone number?

The phone was ringing and a man answered, "Hello." I began to tell him who I was and why I was calling. I told him that the television show had been what prompted me and that I was just wondering how the crab lady was doing. I was a bit embarrassed to say that I couldn't remember her name but that I had saved the number under crab lady. He told me her name was Mary Ann and then he said, "Let me let you talk to her and she can tell you how she's doing."

My emotions were high as I waited for her to come to the phone. She thanked me for calling and then told me all that happened when she went to the doctor. She told me that she asked her doctor to do another scan after we had prayed with her. She said that her cancer was completely gone and that she was so thankful. She said that about a week after we stopped to pray with her, another woman stopped and said that God had sent her to pray with her. Mary Ann told me at first she thought it was me coming back for round two of prayers, but then she realized it was an entirely different woman! God is amazing.

What if I had called and found out that the cancer was still there or that she had died? Would it mean that God had not healed her? I think not. One thing that I am certain of is that when we ask for healing, God delights in it and He always heals us. It may not be the physical healing that we get, but He is healing us in many different ways. Emotionally, physically or spiritually, it doesn't matter. We pray for it all with expectant faith and then we leave the result up to him.

Another point I want to bring out here is that we should always stop and pray with people right then and there. How many people are like the crab lady just waiting for someone to pray with them? How many people would say: **I've been waiting for you**? As I finish this prayer story, I want to say that I called her again this past year and she is still cancer free! To God be the glory! As Kenny and I recall this special time, we both fill with tears and ask ourselves how did this happen? I pray that God is being glorified in the telling of this story. A few more things I want to point out is that this woman had faith, the fisherman had faith, and we had faith. Everyone's faith has been elevated because we obeyed. God says that as believers we will do even greater things than he did. We need more people praying for healing with belief that God will do the healing. We don't have to worry about what we are to say because its God doing the work, we are only vessels. Many people believe in their heads that God can heal, but in their hearts there is doubt that he will. We should use every means to be healed; doctors and medicine but instead of placing all our faith in modern medicine let's go to the divine physician first!

Now let me tell you about my son-in-law Ben who married our youngest daughter Abbey a little over two years ago. When I was in my 30s and attending Bible Study Fellowship, I was taught the importance of praying for your children's future spouse. I can say that I faithfully prayed for all of my kids in this area, but Abbey was the youngest so she got the longest benefit of this type of prayer.

I had many qualities that I asked for in a future husband. Kenny prayed for her as well. As her father, I think he wanted her to have someone who would love, care for her and protect her. This story has two parts. One that I want to share is how we saw our prayer being answered by bringing Ben into Abbey's life. If I checked off the qualities we wanted for Abbey's future husband to have, Ben would have those as well as many more.

The whole way the Lord brought Ben to Abbey was like a fairy tale. I think that Abbey was starting to believe that her dream guy didn't exist. The very week that she was losing hope was the week that Ben showed up. It was New Year's Eve and only God could have orchestrated this last-minute date. Within a very short time, I knew he was the one she would marry. Their courtship accelerated and a year later they were engaged.

That's a very abbreviated story of answered prayer. The greater part of this prayer story will be about how the power of God's word brings life and healing. Ben had told Abbey that he was born with a Ventricular Septal Defect, but that it wasn't too big of a deal. The doctors had told him to get checked regularly, but that his problem of having a hole in his heart would probably never require surgery. Like any engaged woman, Abbey wanted to make sure that Ben was in good health. Not because she wanted to be sure he was healthy enough to marry but because she loved him so much and wanted him to be around into their old age. She asked Ben how long it had been since he had seen his cardiologist. When he told her it had been six years, and he should have been seeing him every other year, she asked him to go see his doctor. This is where the story intensifies.

Ben did make an appointment with his cardiologist in late February and by March was shocked to learn that he was going to need open heart surgery. If he delayed the surgery, his aortic valve would eventually need to be replaced, which at his young age would mean more surgeries down the road. They had some serious decisions to face.

They had planned a July wedding but this new development caused them to rethink their marriage date. All this news seemed to be coming very fast. Kenny and I were on our way to meet Ben's parents and to discuss the July wedding plans. At this point, we knew of the new development with his health, but no plans had been changed.

On our way to meet his parents in Hot Springs, the Holy Spirit gave me the thought that they might want to get married sooner. With this in my heart, my phone started ringing and Abbey's name came up on my caller ID. "Mom how close are you to Hot Springs?" When I told her we were close, she said that there was something she needed to tell us and that she would prefer it wasn't over the phone, but she didn't want us to get to Hot Springs and hear it in conversation and be shocked.

She explained to us that as they thought about the surgery with Ben's mom and dad, they felt like they wanted to get married before the surgery. I wasn't a bit surprised as the Lord had prepared me for this news already. She said we'll still go to the beach and recommit our vows but we think this is the best thing for us to do right now.

They both explained that they wanted Abbey to have rights as a spouse with a say in Ben's surgery and his recovery. With deep love and concern in her heart, Abbey wanted to take care of Ben after his surgery. In the event something might go wrong, Abbey would be cared for as well. They both were willing to give up their dreams for their big wedding for a simple wedding at Ben's Harbor Town Square apartment.

Not only were Abbey and Ben's dreams changing for their desired wedding, so were mine and Kenny's. We had wanted to see Abbey marry in our church with many friends and family. It was very important to her daddy and me for her to have a sacred covenant marriage. This was not for show, but to honor the sacrament of marriage and our Lord.

The day they got married, those present were Ben's parents; his sister Emily; Anthony, Abbey's brother; Tara her sister, and Tara's two girls Channing and Maddie; and Kenny and myself. We drove three hours with a bouquet, some finger foods, a couple of bottles of champagne, and all our love to offer them for their very simple wedding. We prayed the rosary as we traveled. Upon arrival, we visited and then scrambled around to find some candles for their little patio to decorate for the wedding. Ben's family brought a cake.

The tension Abbey and Ben felt was palpable. It wasn't because they were in doubt, but there was so much ahead of them. Abbey looked beautiful in the dress she had found a few days before and

Ben looked handsome as well! Never have I seen such tenderness and love in a wedding ceremony. In my mind, I was certain that this would be just a civil ceremony, but I was so wrong. Abbey had contacted someone from the phonebook and to our surprise as the ceremony started "Reverend Patricia" began to read scripture and the presence of the Lord became very powerful. We witnessed a holy covenant without all the trappings of a big wedding. It was an amazingly beautiful wedding!

The apartment was on Mud Island in Memphis so we just went out the door and down a few doors to the River Inn hotel for some food and drinks afterward. As we entered the lobby, a man was at a piano playing Eric Clapton's "You Look Wonderful Tonight." We all stopped and said, "Here's your opportunity for your first dance." Everyone stopped and watched with tear-filled eyes. Our hearts were full of joy as we knew that only God can make things like that happen!

As a gift from Ben's parents, they spent their honeymoon at the Peabody in Memphis and then went to LeBonheur Children's Hospital the next morning. This was the hospital where Abbey was employed as a child life specialist.

There are so many "God" details to this story. The morning of his surgery came quickly with many family members present. Abbey and Jo, Ben's mom, went back to see Ben before the surgery and the doctor said I have good news and bad news. The bad news is that the hole in Ben's heart was bigger than the doctor thought, but the good news was that he said and I quote: "The hole is shaped like a fish so we may be able to stitch it instead of patching it." Abbey coined the phrase that Ben had a "holey" heart.

It was truly obvious that Jesus was with Ben when we were told the hole was shaped like a fish, the symbol for Christ. The surgery lasted about four hours. The doctor came out and told us that all went well and he would be in intensive care for a while. Once he got to his special room in CICU, the nurse assigned to Ben explained about all the tubes and machines he was connected to. She told us that it would be several hours before Ben would be able to breathe on his own; for now the machine was doing his breathing. She showed us on the screens what it would look like when he took breaths on his own.

It was a scary sight to see Ben hooked up to so many machines and tubes. We sat there and looked at him. The steady rhythm of the machines was a sure reminder of the seriousness of his surgery. We were all concerned, but we were told that he had done well in the surgery. I am a firm believer in using God's word when praying for people. On the way to the hospital that morning Kenny and I were praying for him and after praying I began a word search in scripture that pertained to the heart. I read them one by one but when I got to **Psalm 57:7 KJV** I knew I had found the scripture to use in prayer for Ben. **My heart is fixed, O God, my heart is fixed: I will sing and give praise!** Could there have been a more perfect verse for this situation?

I put it on my Facebook page and asked all those who read my post to pray and claim that for Ben's healing. We were thanking God in advance for what we knew he would do! So, as we watched the respirator do his breathing, I asked Abbey if she had seen the verse I had put on the wall. As she was about to answer, I just spoke it out loud to her in the room: *"My heart is fixed, Oh God, my heart is fixed: I will sing and give praise."*

What happen next was unbelievable. As the word was proclaimed, Ben sat up in his bed and nodded his head in agreement to the Bible verse. As he sat up, he took a few breaths on his own and then when he laid back down, the machine took back over. It was way too soon for him to take any breaths on his own. He was still under very heavy anesthesia from his surgery as well as strong pain medication. His private nurse, his mom Jo, Abbey and I just looked on with amazement. God's word had brought life to him. I will never forget what I saw that day. What are you needing God to bring to life for you?

Ben's surgery was more than two years ago and he is doing wonderfully. He and Abbey have their first baby and his name is Benjamin.

I ask you to allow God to fix your heart. I am challenging you to keep your heart fixed on God. He is able to do amazing things.

My next story is short but equally amazing. While at work one day, my client was spilling out things within her that had happened and that she needed inner healing. As she talked, I knew that God was asking me to pray with her. There was no one in the salon at the time but the two of us. It's customary for me to put the radio on when I pray with people so that if someone were to come in, the radio would buffer the noise. I asked my client if she would like for me to pray with her and she said yes. I prayed for a few minutes and I felt the Lord telling me to stop and just listen. So that's what we did. I explained to her that we would just get quiet and listen. I asked her to still herself and listen to the voice of God.

As we sat there, I became aware of the radio, not in too much of a distracting way, but it was definitely audible. My client was getting restless a bit and I again said "let's just be still" and then I realized that the radio was no longer playing. I stayed focused on the prayer and when we finished, I went over to see what had happened to the radio and it was turned off. I said: "Did you notice the radio was off?" As soon as I said that, she was surprised at what had happened. I pondered what the Lord was saying and why He had turned the radio off.

When He says: "be quiet, get still" He means it! It was definitely a work of the Holy Spirit. When the radio turned off on its own, the power of the Lord became very strong. You could feel the presence of the Lord. The Holy Spirit began to download information to both of us. We cannot hear God if we don't get quiet. *"Be still, and know that I am God. I am exalted among the nations, I am exalted in the earth!"* - **Psalm 46:10**

Rosie was a new client for me. The first time she came in the door of Debbie's Hair and Prayer, my heart was touched. She walked with a significant limp and it was obvious that she had suffered some sort of trauma. I immediately knew that the Lord wanted me to minister to her, but I also knew to wait on His lead and not run ahead of the grace.

Her time in my chair would be several hours so I had lots of time to listen to her story. By God's design, we were alone in the salon that day. As I listened to this very beautiful woman tell her story, I saw a strong woman of faith and someone who had been given some very difficult challenges in life. She told me her limp was due to a debilitating stroke. She had been in therapy for quite a while and had regained a lot of strength that the stroke had tried to take from her. It's amazing what the Lord will bring out when someone feels they are in a safe environment. Besides her stroke, she told me of her husband's illness and death, she talked about her son, and she also shared about the loss of her mother.

A few days before she came into the salon, I had gone to Hobby Lobby looking for a gift for my sister in Christ. She loved the song "It Is Well with My Soul," and I found the perfect canvas with those words on it. I was delighted to find it. I placed it in the back seat of my vehicle (which sometimes looks like a traveling messy office on wheels), and it was still in my Tahoe the day that Rosie came in. As she shared about her mother's death, she told me about her friend singing at her mother's funeral. She said that she had sung: "It Is Well with My Soul" and tears filled her eyes as she spoke of it.

As I listened, I knew immediately that the canvas wasn't for my friend, but for Rosie! All I can say is that God is amazing, and he is in the small details as well as the big things in our lives. I would give her the plaque at the right time.

As I listened, I would ask a question here and there. When I asked her if she had found a church home, she told me that she hadn't, but that she was looking for one. After I felt that she had covered most of the things that were on her heart, I asked her if it would be OK to pray with her. One thing I remember praying about with her was to find a church home. We also prayed for continued healing in her body, soul and spirit. As we prayed for several different things, I knew the Lord was ministering to her because the tears were flowing. This is usually a sign of the Holy Spirit's presence. Her time with me was finished and she loved her hair.

The Lord has shown me that I have been gifted to be a great hairdresser because He has need of me in the marketplace. My gifting and the spirit of God within me would bring her back. When it was time for her to pay, I asked her to excuse me so I could go out to my traveling office on wheels. Joy was bubbling out of me because I knew that I was going to walk in with the gift of the canvas that had the very words "It Is Well with My Soul" written on it. When I got back inside, I told her that I had a gift for her. I know she was taken back for a moment, but as soon as she pulled it out from the sack, she knew that God was touching her heart in a very personal way. As we shared that moment, I explained to her that I thought I had bought it for my friend, but that the Lord had her in mind when I purchased it. The story doesn't end there.

On her next visit, she was so excited to tell me that she had found a church home! It felt just right to her. She told me about the things she liked about it and thanked me for praying with her. We visited and chatted about her new church. She wanted to get involved, but wasn't sure how the Lord would use her. I asked her about her gifts and she spoke of past things she had done in her church before moving to Conway. One was a youth leader. She also told me that prior to her stroke, she had played the piano but couldn't anymore. Besides she said, "They have a pianist."

We prayed for her to find her place of gifting in her church. So now we are into another visit in the salon and she was spilling over telling me that the pianist was leaving. She looked me square in the eye and said: "I want to play the piano again. I want to be the pianist for my new church!" My reply was: "Why not you? We're going to pray that the Lord heals that part of your brain and body."

She practiced diligently every day in a church where there was no air conditioning on during the day. This was a real sacrifice for her. Without going into all the details, it wasn't long before God provided a piano for her home. No longer would she have to leave her home every day nor would she be in the heat at her church.

And pray we did! Only a few weeks had past and I got a call from her with the best news. She said: "Debbie, I'm playing the piano!" I was thrilled beyond words. She had overcome her limitations and was playing at her church. God had healed her in another area. Isn't God good?

CHAPTER 9

UNANSWERED PRAYER: OR IS IT?

Is there such a thing as unanswered prayer? What do you think? What happens when we pray and we see no immediate results? I struggle with this one and I'm sure that you do too.

What the Holy Spirit has taught me is that God is God and I am not. God teaches us this in the story of Job. Reading all the book of Job helped me to see that I don't have the right to tell God what to do. We can question God, I suppose, because that is what a real relationship is like, but in the end, we, like Job, must put our hand over our mouth and silence ourselves. *"I am unworthy—how can I reply to you? I put my hand over my mouth." -* **Job 40:4**

Like Job we must say *"I know that thou canst do all things, and that no purpose of thine can be thwarted. 3 'Who is this that hides counsel without knowledge?' Therefore I have uttered what I did not understand things too wonderful for me, which I did not know. 4 'Hear, and I will speak; I will question you, and you declare to me.' 5 I had heard of thee by the hearing of the ear, but now my eye sees thee; 6 therefore I despise myself, and repent in dust and ashes." -* **Job 42: 2-6**

Currently, I am in a prayer battle for our son Anthony. About a year ago, he started having some strange symptoms. After many trips to many different doctors, we learned that Anthony had Psoriatic Arthritis. This can be a debilitating disease if not treated properly. Treatment drugs can cause other problems besides the initial disease. All of the what-ifs can send you into a dark place. Each trip to the doctor brings more to process and discern. It can consume your every breath and thought. It can be a long period of unknowns and all you can do is take one day at a time. You surrender to God then you take it back the next day. Over and over you pray and hope for the good news, but it doesn't come in the way you wanted.

I'm sure that many of you who are reading this have had some diagnoses that have nearly swamped you. I struggled with the whys and am still trying to process all this. I asked the Blessed Mother "Why my son?" and she replied back to me: "Why my son?" I asked our heavenly Father: "Why my son?" And He replied back: "Why my son?" As I watched my 33-year-old son and his wife walk through this dark valley, I ran straight to the Father in fear and tears. One would think that after following the Lord closely for over 30 plus years you would not succumb to the plots of the enemy, fear and worry so easily. The truth is that he uses the same tactics over and over and when you begin to know this, you may be deceived for a bit, but you quickly recognize it and get back to true north. Everything that I knew about healing was now being brought to a new level of knowing.

It's hard to find out that you have a disease that man says is incurable; but God's history has proven over and over again that he is a healing God. I have also come to know that it is not God's will for us to be sick. If it was that way, why did Jesus take time to heal the sick? Sickness entered into our world at the fall of our first parents, Adam and Eve, but as we read further into scripture, Jesus brings life and healing,

He sent His word and healed them, And delivered them from their destructions.

—Psalm 107:20.

But He was wounded for our transgressions, He was bruised for our iniquities; The chastisement for our peace was upon Him, And by His stripes we are healed.

—Isaiah 53:5

Jesus is the face of the Father here on earth. Yes, God filters everything through His fingertips and He can heal immediately and He does, but what about the times He doesn't? And how can a good God allow suffering and sickness in the first place?

So what might block healing? Faith is one key ingredient in healing. Why ask for healing if we really don't expect it or if we believe that we don't deserve it? If we don't receive a physical healing, does that mean we lacked faith? In some cases the answer may be yes, but many times I think we just don't know all that God is doing. We can't see the whole picture. We want to believe but our faith is weak.

Another area that could possibly block our healing prayers can be that of unforgiveness. Have you been the victim of an unforgivable situation? Were you the one who caused the unforgivable situation? Harboring this pain in your heart is like having heavy chains upon you. Chains that are so heavy, you can't even move. These chains effect every part of every day. Maybe you're not even aware of how bound up you are. You are shackled in a prison that you have the key to open but, sometimes, the pain is just too much to work through, so we stay in our prison because at least its familiar to us.

These chains may even have caused you to die a spiritual death. You are like Lazarus who had been dead for three days, bound in the burial cloths and you've been like this so long, there is a stench. Jesus is saying to you: "Come out. I am bringing you back to life if you will let me." Our shackles can sometimes be small ones, yet they still block our healing. As you read this, is something coming to the surface that you need to deal with? Is there a stench because you are slowly decaying from the hurt? Is there some area of unforgiveness? Abuse, neglect, rejection, and bullying, for example, can all cause so much pain and dysfunction.

Please, stop right now and ask God for the grace to help you extend mercy and forgiveness to those who have harmed you. If you have been the one who has hurt the other, ask God for the grace to approach them for their forgiveness.

I have come to realize that we only see a partial picture of what God is doing. If suffering was not necessary, Jesus would have removed himself from the cross. He stayed to show us the way of suffering and its redemptive value. Suffering produces holiness and wholeness in ourselves and others. It is in suffering that we become truly dependent on God and we grow in humility and holiness.

I am also sure that when we ask for healing, God always heals. Sometimes it is not in the way that we wanted, but God always extends healing. In my opinion, the greater healing is inner healing. All of Jesus' healing ministry pointed not only to a physical healing, but a much deeper healing interiorly. While waiting on healing, suffering can produce great graces for others as well. Paul sums it up well. *Now I rejoice in my sufferings for your sake, and in my flesh I complete what is lacking in Christ's afflictions for the sake of his body, that is, the church, - Colossians 1:24*

What does this mean? I believe the following remarks from Mark Shea in the *National Catholic Register* express this scripture well. He states: "Of course, God doesn't 'need' our sufferings any more than he needs our money. He's complete and overflows with life. The universe was not made out of need, but out of gift. Our sufferings are therefore part of the gift he makes to us, weird as that sounds. As to 'lack' the term doesn't refer to God lacking anything, nor to some inadequacy on Christ's part but to our lack. For instance, God is the giver of all things and intends us to have all we need. Yet, in this world, people experience lack every day. Why? In no small part because we (who are entrusted with the task of distributing what is needed for the common good) don't supply the lack. So people starve or go thirsty. Is that because there is a lack on the part of the author of Being? No!

"In the same way, Christ's sacrifice is sufficient. But since he has made us participants in that sacrifice, our acts of sacrifice 'matter' too. Had the apostles failed to proclaim the gospel, we would not have heard about it. We would lack. If somebody had not told me about Jesus, I would lack. If I don't make the sacrifice of time to (for instance) reply to your note, you don't get an answer to your question. You lack, not because Christ is insufficient, but because I don't discharge my duty of trying to help. I don't 'offer my body a living sacrifice' you therefore don't receive the benefits of Christ's sacrifice in the form of a letter from a brother in Christ who might have helped, but didn't. You lack, not because of Jesus' inadequacy, but because of mine.

"I'm hoping that makes sense. The bottom line is: Christ mediates his grace to us through creatures, especially other people. We have nothing to offer God by ourselves. Even our ability to say yes is a gift of grace. But God has so willed that we can indeed make that offering—or not. When we do, it is joined to Christ's offering and becomes part of the gift he makes of himself to the Church. The same is true of the mysterious sufferings of those who, seemingly, have nothing to offer but suffering. From a practical and utilitarian viewpoint, a bedridden victim of some disease appears to have 'nothing to offer.' But then, so did Jesus when he hung on the cross and, to utilitarian eyes, accomplished nothing useful for six hours. In fact, of course, he accomplished the redemption of the world.

A suffering soul likewise can join his or her sufferings to Jesus and, in his mysterious exchange of love, do great and wonderful things for others." So, sickness or suffering or what we think of as unanswered prayer can bring about much more than we can ever imagine."

Praying for healing is not just a one-time prayer. Healing prayer needs to be a saturating daily prayer. If you have been given a diagnosis that man says is incurable, keep praying in hope. The enemy would love to block your prayers by making you think your prayers aren't working or that it's impossible for you to be healed. Besides praying, link up with other believers who have faith in healing prayer. They can help you when you get discouraged and remind you of the truth that God's word says. We pray with expectant faith that God will heal us. We use all means for that to happen; medicine, doctors, and saturating prayer, then we leave the outcome to our Papa.

As I am writing about this journey with my son and his wife, I'm plucking all the graces that we are receiving along the way. It seems like with each new battle this situation is bringing, God raises the standard.

> *So shall they fear the name of the Lord from the west,*
> *and his glory from the rising of the sun. When the enemy*
> *shall come in like a flood, the Spirit of the Lord shall lift*
> *up a standard against him.*

—Isaiah 59:19 KJV

As Anthony and Meridee offer their sufferings, I too offer my part of suffering in this as well. What affects one person in my family, affects the rest of us. So it is in the body of Christ. Whether we know it or not, we are in the body of Christ and we are all affected by what others in the body undergo.

I am being pruned and reformed just as they are. I am learning about hope in God alone. God is deepening my awareness that He ultimately wants our good. He is for us not against us! We know this in our heads but do we really believe it? I cannot imagine what a mother or father must feel like when they must bury their child. The last thing that I want you to be thinking here is that you didn't pray hard enough or you didn't have faith enough or that you didn't do something correct in the formula for healing. The bottom line is that we pray in expectant faith but we hope in God alone. We hold our will loosely and choose to **trust** God.

> *What then shall we say to this? If God is for us,*
> *who is against us?*

—Romans 8:31

WHEN OUR PRAYER DOES NOT produce the results we want, we enter into a death of our will or ego. It is a pruning in such a way that when we offer it to the Lord, it becomes beautiful; a crucifixion of our wants and desires and a submission to the ultimate good that God wants to bring out of it. It is an interior martyrdom. We become detached to our control of the situation and learn to dwell in the now and can say as Paul:

> *"Not that I complain of want; for I have learned, in*
> *whatever state I am, to be content. 12 I know how to*
> *be abased, and I know how to abound; in any and all*
> *circumstances I have learned the secret of facing plenty*
> *and hunger, abundance and want.*
> *13 I can do all things in him who strengthens me.*

—Philippians 4:11-13

So for now in regard to my son Anthony, I keep praying and trusting God and know that He has the best plan. I can see that the doctors, medicine, and faith are all working together to give Anthony a great quality of life and hope for a very healthy future. Anthony and Meridee have grown immensely in this journey. I am certain their faith is stronger and that this time of testing is producing great holiness. For sure, God will be glorified in all of this!

IF WE ARE HONEST with ourselves, how many of us can say that, after we have prayed so fervently for something that we didn't get, the outcome of God's will or plan was much better than we could have ever imagined? This is the stance of faith and the grace of acceptance. We wait patiently and we accept with gratitude that gift which came to us wrapped in not-so-pretty paper but had a blessing inside. I have such an example that comes to my mind here! May I share another one of my life's stories?

Twenty-two years ago, I was in my office at the Catholic Diocese of Little Rock. If you recall in my earlier chapters, I was the Executive Director for the Cursillo movement in Arkansas. One beautiful gifting of the day-to-day working there was the beautiful chapel that I could go to on any given day. I usually spent some of my lunch time sitting with Jesus. It was a beautiful October day and things were going well in my family. We were as busy as cranberry merchants at harvest time (a saying of my dad's). I had been to the chapel and upon returning to my office the phone was blinking signaling that I had a new voice mail message. I picked up the phone to retrieve it and I had a message from our 18-year-old daughter. It went something like this: "Mom, I'm coming to Little Rock, I need to talk to you." This was not a normal voice mail message. My office was thirty miles from our home and it was most unusual that Tara would call and want to make a trip to talk to me in the middle of the day. While I didn't hear anxiety in her voice, my mother alarm began to sound. I immediately heard the Lord tell me to go back to the chapel. Thankfully I followed His lead.

As I sat in the chapel for only a few minutes I clearly heard Him say to me in an interior voice: "Tara is going to tell you she's pregnant." My first reaction was that of fear and some disbelief as she had only been seeing Jason for about three months; but I received that word from the Lord and began to pray. Many thoughts were flying around in my mind, but the most important prayer I prayed was: "Lord help me to respond in love to whatever I hear from Tara." I sat there for about 10 minutes and a peace settled over me. I knew it was about time for her to arrive so I went back to my office to wait. As the door to my office opened, there stood my beautiful daughter. She burst into tears and said: "Mom, I'm pregnant." As I remember, I ran to her and we hugged and I said: "I know. It's going to be alright. Why don't we go to the chapel and let's talk there?"

We sat before Jesus, and with Jesus for the next thirty minutes or so and many things came out. My heart was heavy, I cannot lie, but I knew that our family would do whatever it took to support our daughter. It really doesn't matter what all was said because I don't remember all of it for sure, but what I do remember was that I knew that we would all be OK.

I'm sure as you are reading this, some of you faced this same situation. Maybe it was you that had to tell your mom that you were pregnant or it was your daughter or son that said this to you. Stay with your thoughts right here and listen for a moment for some healing that the Lord might want to do with you.

Tara and I walked out of that chapel two different people. I had no anger in my heart and I believe that she felt loved and protected. The first person that I saw as I left the chapel was Barbara, who had gone through the same thing years earlier. God always provides just what we need and he is always right on time. Tara left and I had an opportunity to get the first word of encouragement from another Christian mother who had already walked where I was walking. I went back to my office with so many thoughts running through my head.

Have you ever been in a place where you had no idea what the future could possibly bring? Actually, each new day can bring an unimaginable change that was never asked for or perceived. After speaking a few minutes to my friend, I called my mother-in-law. I had to tell someone. Verna was always calm and certainly had the habit of reacting in love. There was a deep concern in my heart how Kenny would handle the news that his daughter was pregnant. Verna listened intently on the other end of the line as I asked her for prayers for all of us; but especially Kenny. I didn't want him to explode with anger and I just didn't know how this would play out. Verna wanted to come to Conway with Ken, my father-in-law, but I asked them to just pray and let us try and process this privately at first. As we hung up the phone, I made one more phone call before leaving for home. "Hey babe, can you come home from work early? I need to talk to you about something. I should be home in about 45 minutes."

I was sitting on our front porch swing praying, when Kenny rounded the corner into our cul-de-sac. My heart was racing with lots of fear. As I look back, this actually saddens me. How could I have ever thought that a father like Kenny could abandon or react in anger toward one of his children? He sat next to me on the swing as I told him about Tara. I will never forget how he responded. Pure love came over him and his fatherly protection kicked in. He said things like: "Tara can raise the baby here, we will help her anyway she needs help. We will even raise the baby if we need to." His reaction was that of pure love. We were under a mantle of abundant grace. Not only did that happen, but no sooner than I had told Kenny, I looked up and Kenny's mom and dad were pulling up. Even though I asked them not to come, they wanted to show their solidarity with us in this whole situation. We would face this as a family together! I have to add here that Jason's family also rallied to help in many wonderful ways. We all worked together as a team!

There were many days ahead that reality tried to kick us in the behind. My approach was to just put the truth out into the open. We did not try to hide this beautiful gift from God in a package of shame, but instead, let the light of Christ shine out into the places ahead that seemed to bring uncertainty or fear. My clients in my salon were watching and listening to what I was saying and doing concerning this situation. I was very vocal about being pro-life. Would my actions line up with my words? I had many women tell me that they wished their mother's would have responded to them in this way.

Let me be totally transparent right here. The Lord gave me many odd shaped gifts. I was learning to not worry about the future, how to let go, how to release worry, how to love unconditionally, how to be merciful and how to be loving and forgiving, but the one that was very valuable to me at this time was that of being humbled and about the serious conviction of judging people.

We all want our families to be perfect and I am no different. The truth is that we all have dysfunctions and shortcomings, but heaven forbid if someone knows that. In our world of social media we paint the image of perfection. Imagine a Norman Rockwell image of the perfect Thanksgiving meal or Christmas celebration. Is that what your family really looks like?

Up to this point in our family life, I actually thought I had the perfect family and I was very proud of it. I had done such a marvelous job. I, I, I! This pregnancy news would blow our image. Not only that, but the Holy Spirit started making me think about the many times I had judged other young ladies who were, in my opinion, promiscuous. Surely their mothers had not taught them well enough. I was leveled to humility and my false pride was being toppled over. I had to repent and face my own shortcomings and failures. I had to see, with eyes of mercy, all those I had formed judgmental opinions about. Not only did I have to deal with having judged people but Kenny and I had to take responsibility for the part we played in this situation.

I was brought to the verses in *Matthew 7:1-3 "Judge not, that you be not judged. 2 For with the judgment you pronounce you will be judged, and the measure you give will be the measure you get. 3 Why do you see the speck that is in your brother's eye, but do not notice the log that is in your own eye?*

Suddenly, I was before the only judge who matters. It was God the Father and He dealt with me gently but firmly. He showed me that mistakes and poor judgement can happen. He showed me areas that I had acted impurely in my youth. He showed me that I needed to repent and walk forth in humility. He also showed me that I could be grateful that we were not facing the horrors of an abortion, but even that choice deserves God's mercy. I was even called to confess my guilt of judging and pride to individuals in my salon when the Lord told me to do so. I thank God for these lessons to this day. Although I didn't realize it at the time, these many gifts brought more and more interior freedom. The image of perfection was just too hard to live up to. Perfectionism is the birthplace of shame. This would not be the last time that I would have to open the gift of humility and judgmentalism.

I remember telling Tara one day that I had dreams for her and that I was having to surrender my dreams for this place of reality. I will never forget what she said back to me. "Mom, I have dreams too. They're just coming sooner that I thought they would. I've always wanted to get married and have a baby. It's just happening sooner than I expected."

When you are expecting your first grandchild, you have dreams that it would happen a certain way, but God allowed this dream to be transformed into one that caused great growth in our entire family. We would never have made it without the grace of God and friends and the family members who stood beside us. As in any difficult situation, we learned to just take it one day at a time.

My constant prayer for Jason, who was 17, and Tara, who was 18, was that truth would be spoken between them. I didn't know what should happen for them. This was their life and their journey. Kenny and I didn't want to force marriage or block it. We just wanted them to be honest with each other about what they were really feeling and we wanted to help them achieve their hearts' desires. If you have been in difficult places with your young adult children, you know how hard it is to let go and allow them to plunge headfirst into the future. We cannot allow the what-ifs to take control of our minds and lose the grace of the present moment.

To say that from the fall of 1996 to the spring of 1998 was a difficult year and a half would be a tremendous understatement. I think that there wasn't an emotion that could be felt that Kenny and I didn't have. You see, we had our oldest son get married in April, our grandson Parker was born in June, Tara and Jason got married in September, my mom and dad were aged parents who's health had declined in such a way that it had caused tremendous strain on my siblings and myself, our financial situation was pretty bleak, and there was internal strife in our extended family over all of these things. If this wasn't enough, my precious daddy died shortly thereafter. As I recall this year, I know that it was one of the times in my life that I experienced the most stretching and difficulty, but it became one of the times that I look back on and know that I experienced the most growth.

June 6, 1997, came and it was the feast day of the Sacred Heart of Jesus. I had prayed that my grandson would be born on this day and the Lord gave me the desires of my heart. I had also prayed that he would feel the love we all had for him in the womb and after he was born. My other prayer was that he would be full of joy. As I watched his birth happening, I was filled with awe, love and peace. They placed Parker in his mother's arms and the first time I saw him eye-to-eye he smiled at me! God was showing me he had heard my heartfelt prayers. This child was full of joy! He knew he was loved.

Now 22 years later, this package that came delivered as a gift in not-so-pretty paper has proven to be one powerful story of grace and transformation. Not just for Jason and Tara, but Kenny and me as well. How does this story relate to prayers not being answered or the way we want them to? I had prayed for Tara to have the storybook version of courtship and marriage. My prayers were answered, but not in the way I wanted or thought they should be.

As I am typing away, Tara and Jason just left our house for the airport for a new adventure, moving 23 hours away to their new home in Utah. They have been married for 20 years and have four beautiful children. Parker is now a junior in college and the fears and what-ifs never materialized. I couldn't be prouder of their family. Jason grew from a 17-year-old boy bagging groceries into one heck of a man, father and husband. Tara is the mom I dreamed of, only better. They have overcome the struggles of their early years and Jason has built a career over the last 20 years that is putting him into an upper level management position in the grocery business. This all happened without him earning a college degree and I am well pleased with both of them.

Yes, my heart must once again let go of my desires and dreams as they move so far away, but history has taught me that God sends presents that we wouldn't pick, but have just the right contents in them. I stated earlier that I thought we had the perfect family. I still think so. We are perfectly imperfect and that's a great thing!

So when you're praying for healing, finances, relationships, or any imaginable thing, know that God does answer you in His omnipotent ways and in His time frame. Don't be afraid to open His gifts! He is worth being trusted with all of your prayers.

⋟⊹⊱

CHAPTER 10
DYING ONCE AGAIN

Humility always radiates the greatness and
glory of God.
How wonderful are the ways of God! He used
humility, smallness, helplessness
and poverty to prove to the world that
He loved the world.
Let us not be afraid to be humble, small and
helpless to prove our love to God.

—St. Mother Teresa

Has the Lord humbled you? It could be that you've never experienced being humbled. Are you in a situation that you are experiencing a dose of humility right now? The testimonies I have shared all brought a plethora of graces and responses, but this particular one is where I truly experienced a slow difficult death and a life-giving dose of humility. Mine was not a physical death but one in which my ego was stripped and was a death to my ways and will. Even as I type, I know that I must be fully transparent, which takes humility.

As you have journeyed with me through these pages, I hope that there has been a renewed faith and trust in God. When we pray for certain things, we must be ready to undergo the processes that God must bring us through to get us to the desired place. This story is one such example. It will also show the importance of having a spiritual director and a resolve to plow through the dirt and muck of life with the grace of God. When we get to the hard places, it's nearly impossible to go it alone.

Kenny and I have always had to work hard to earn a living. Being self-employed has many perks but it also brings stress and other undesired results. Because we were both self-employed for most of our married years, we were forced to learn the life lesson of divine providence to keep our sanity. Sometimes, we did well in knowing this and other times we entered into fear and worry. It took me many years to realize that we weren't the providers: it was all God and His provisions.

With each passing year, we learned to lean on God a bit more. It seemed that we always had enough, but never a big surplus. As far as savings, we never were able to have very much. We managed to put our four kids through Catholic school and had a few luxuries like family vacations and the things that teenagers felt were necessities. Our home was large and in its time was a showcase, but more importantly it was a home in the sheltering sense of the word. We were able to have it because Kenny put lots of sweat equity in it. I have to admit that I am proud of our home and God has allowed us to keep this home now for 31 years.

My early pride was showy; the pride I have now is gratitude. One thing we wanted from the first day that we moved into the house was for it to be a place of hospitality for our family and for God's servants. I believe that we have honored God with this home in just that way.

Our work ethic was strong and we earned our living by the sweat of our brow. Neither one of us were lazy or afraid of hard work. As a hairdresser, I stood many long days on my feet and dealt with all kinds of egos and insecurities in my clients as well as my own prideful ego. Kenny worked hard in the elements of heat or freezing temperatures building homes. We both had to deal with employees and the pressures of not only making an income for our own family but being successful enough to keep our employees gainfully employed. This brought about stress as well. My business really never suffered much through the different ebbs and flows of recessions. In fact, I opened my business in one of the most volatile financial times in the last 30 years. I thank God so very much that my income was always stable and pretty reliable. I also thank Him for the talent He gave me to be successful.

Kenny's business however was always driven by the pulse of the economy. It was always feast or famine. I actually remember one day in my salon when one of my clients asked me if I was afraid of the upcoming financial crisis that was looming. I proudly stated that we were always blessed to weather the storms and that I wasn't too worried. In time, that statement would come back to haunt me. Maybe there was some sense of pride in my answer.

Building homes and doing the actual labor of these projects eventually can take a toll on your body. As we were both aging, the physical labor we were doing became harder each year. There came a time when it was clear that Kenny had to make some changes to accommodate the physical and emotional strains his work was having on him. We decided together that he would start to scale down from the physical demands of framing and having crews to a smaller scale of remodeling. We thought that this would help him to make a comfortable income and not have as much strain on his body. With the completion of each new project we were always looking for God to provide the next one. God always provided just in the nick of time.

Things were moving along pretty well and then we hit the recession. We had kids in college and work wasn't coming in. Banks were collapsing right and left due to poor loans and improper protocol. Credit card companies began raising interest rates on existing cards that were supposed to have locked in interest rates. The housing market began to fall. Homes were being foreclosed on all over the country. As a result, residential home builders in our areas started doing remodeling to survive. This cut into the work Kenny would have been getting and thus began our downward spiral and loss of income.

We scaled back in as many areas as we could but as things got worse, it became increasingly harder to pay our bills. Again, I was so thankful for my business as the Lord seemed to keep that a constant for us. I want to believe that He blessed my business because I was honoring Him there. This is not to say Kenny's business was not God-honoring, but my business had become a place of ministry. As I mentioned in earlier chapters, my salon was known as "Debbie's Hair and Prayer." Even so, I even felt some lean years due to bizarre circumstances of employees leaving. It seemed that the enemy was trying to sabotage my business because he wanted to stop the evangelization that was happening there. The more he tried, the more I dug in and prayed.

We began to experience longer periods of underemployment for Kenny and we started going deeper and deeper into debt. I could tell this situation was making me angry. I hate to admit it, but I had thoughts in my head that this was all Kenny's fault, when in fact, I had a part to play in the whole situation as well. It's easy to look to others and blame them when the Lord wants you to look inward.

It was around this time that I started going to spiritual direction, and it proved to be a life preserver for me during a time when I felt that I couldn't breathe and I was drowning. One particular visit Fr. Mark said that the things I was telling him reminded him of a book he had read called *Breathing Underwater* by Richard Rohr. While I didn't get the book until a year later, the title just captivated me and ministered to me. I would hear, breathing underwater, breathing underwater at different times and I would imagine what that book was about. It seemed to me that there must be a way to keep breathing when you feel like you're drowning. This book title became a mantra for me. I would tell myself, "just keep breathing, Debbie."

Let me insert here that a few years before this downturn happened, I was getting thoughts that I was not going to live long. I felt that the Lord was preparing me for death. Little did I know that I was being prepared for death, but it was my ego or false self that had to die. Our dear Lord wanted me to enter into new life and to have this happen, I needed to carry the cross, die to my false self, and enter into the new resurrected me.

Truly, truly, I say to you, unless a grain of wheat falls into the earth and dies, it remains alone; but if it dies, it bears much fruit.

—John 12:24

The beginning of this death to ego started in my first eight-day silent retreat that I wrote about earlier. I experienced that gift of breaking down at the "bearing tree" but it was something that took many years of month-after-month spiritual direction to break through to my true core self. Each month I would walk into Fr. Mark's office and only a few minutes into the hour of direction, I would be crying. It was very hard for me to admit how dire our situation was. I was embarrassed and, I guess you could say, I felt shame. As I look back, I know this was the enemy bringing those feelings to me. There is no shame in losing your income or things, but in our society, many of us value ourselves by the money we make and the things we own.

God was showing me that I, too, had a disordered attachment to money. Monetary success doesn't define who you are. My whole way of seeing was being recalibrated. Some of this focus or view on money was a learned behavior from my upbringing. My family had everything we needed but, as I reflect back, my mother and father had to work very hard to provide for us, My mother was one of 17 children. Only 14 of her siblings made it to adulthood. Her father died when she was eight and this was during the depression. Mama said they nearly starved to death. They ate potatoes for almost every meal, so she became very focused on money and not having enough. Her fear of not having enough to provide carried into her adulthood and I inherited it. I'm not passing the blame, just pointing out that we learn many of our adult behaviors while we are children.

While we were undergoing this financial trial, if there was a bit of leftovers, I made good use of them. When I went to the grocery store, I found myself praying in the spirit (in charismatic tongues) as I walked down the aisles. I did this so I would find the bargains and not get things I didn't need. Praying in the spirit also lifted my thoughts upward and not on the problem. I also became keenly aware of the less fortunate who do without all the time, so my prayers were for them as well!

Some weeks I could only buy food for a few days. I found out I didn't need some of the expensive cleaners that I had always purchased. I also found out that many things that I thought we needed were really not important. I would tell Fr. Mark how serious our situation was, but I also began to notice that I was telling him how close to the Lord I was during this time. Each month I would have situations showing how God was leading us and how I could feel his presence. One month turned into two and two turned into six, and, before I knew it, a year had passed and we were still afloat; then, another year and another. Not only was God teaching me about humility, but He was teaching us to look solely to Him for our day-to-day needs. God alone is enough. St. Teresa of Avila says it so well!

Let nothing upset you,
let nothing startle you.
All things pass;
God does not change.
Patience wins
all it seeks.
Whoever has God
lacks nothing:
God alone is enough

- St. Teresa Avila

About a year into this crisis and about a year and a half into spiritual direction, I had discerned that I wanted to become a Spiritual Director. After applying and getting accepted, these monthly weekend trainings began to be an oasis for me. One of my closest friends, Diane, was also in school with me and I would be remiss if I didn't say how valuable her friendship was to me and still is to this day. I could be totally transparent with her and it was always a breath of fresh air to get in the car on Friday afternoon and retreat for 24 hours with her, the Lord, and all my other classmates. Diane and I would talk as fast as we could in that 30-minute drive. Some weeks I talked all the way and other weeks she did the talking. I want to give a shout out to all the wonderful men and women that I was in school with. There were lots of weekends that I was able to take the garbage of my mind, dump it there and drive off. Praise the Lord!

There were many days that I would crumble. This made me so aggravated at myself. I couldn't understand how I could be so worried and agitated with the history I had with God. I felt that my faith should be stronger than what I was exhibiting, yet I would fall into fear and worry. Upon meditating and asking God why these were my responses, I was made aware that this was the sin of pride.

I needed to receive healing. I needed to admit that I needed a savior and always will. I had it in my head that I should be able to do this on my own, but I discovered we all need the mercy of God at all times in our lives.

All along the way of this journey, God provided. He was probably thinking: "What am I going to have to do to get through to her?" May I share two stories that stand out and come to my mind in the middle of the storm?

Now, I don't know if you ladies reading this remember the feather craze that hit the salon industry. I've been a hairdresser for 45 years and I haven't seen another fad that hit the salons like the feather craze! Children, adolescents, college age, young moms, and older women wanted to have a feather or two put in their hair. It only took a few minutes to put them in and you could make a good little chunk of change. The feather craze was just that: crazy!

I found a great supply source and was able to get feathers in when other salons in my area couldn't get them. Word would get out when I received a shipment in and people would run into the salon. Feathers were flying everywhere. The poor chickens that summer! This happened for one whole summer and it patched Kenny and me financially through that season. Thanks, Lord, for chickens!

Another situation that I recall was in December. I'm not sure of the year, but it was well into the famine years. I was driving on my way to see Fr. Mark and talking to my sister-in-law on the phone (which I should not have been doing) about the family Christmas party. The more we talked the faster I drove. I was in a construction zone no less. Before I knew what had happened, I saw blue lights in my rear view mirror. I was so angry at my carelessness and, yes, he gave me a speeding ticket. I could have just screamed. I cried the rest of the way to my appointment.

The police officer told me that he would make it easy on me and my court date would be after Christmas. He also said that if I didn't want to contest it, I could just call and pay over the phone. I put the ticket out of my mind until a few days before that January date.

Now, you know how blue January days can be. I called to see what the fine would be and learned that, since I was in a construction zone, the fine would be doubled and that this particular judge that would hear my case required that you go before him in court. He didn't mess around with construction zones! My court date was a workday which meant not only would the ticket be $350, but I would have to miss a full day's work. I was at home and I fell to the floor sobbing. My son called right at that time and wondered why I was so upset. My pride couldn't tell him how it was impossible for me to lose this much money. I was devastated. I can remember him saying: "Mom, I'm so worried about you." I thought to myself, "If you only knew."

You see I had never told the kids how bad it was. Providentially, right after he called, my dear brother priest friend Fr. John called. He knew what we were going through, in fact, he knows everything about us. He is such a precious dear friend to our family. He has been Jesus to us on so many occasions. I was still crying and I told him what had happened. He told me that he had a great friend who was a lawyer and he might be able to help me. Long story short, he was able to get the fine reduced to just a Saturday of driving school. At this same time, a close friend wrote us a very generous check to help us through this scrape. I might add that she did this on more than one occasion. It was always done in such a beautiful way. It was hard to be on the receiving end, but, you see, God wanted me to be humbled enough to take the money.

There was a particular visit with Fr. Mark when I felt like I had turned a corner. As I sat there I told him how grateful I had become for all the little things that I had taken for granted. I was not angry anymore and my heart was so thankful that we were somehow making it day-to-day. You see, I had always known that

God was my provider, but most of that knowing was in my head. God wanted me to have that knowing in a deeper way. When you come to know something in this way, your word of testimony becomes a lived experience and it is very powerful!

I remember Fr. Mark looked at me and said: "Debbie, this situation has not turned you bitter, it has produced an attitude of gratitude. I'm very happy for you!" I was coming to the realization that I was, indeed, breathing underwater. As well as I was adjusting, however, the situation was only getting worse, but somehow I had gotten to a place of peace.

> *Total surrender means totally abandoning ourselves*
> *into his hands;*
> *yielding totally to his love giving him supreme*
> *freedom over us*
> *to express his love as he pleases, with no thought of self.*

> *—St. Mother Teresa*

It was at this time that I feel like a miracle happened in our lives. Maybe you could say that this was the final straw that broke the camel's back. Kenny's back and mine, that is. Maybe this was the Lord's last test of our obedience. The miracle would take a few weeks to evolve but it started at daily Mass. As I sat in the pew listening to Fr. John's homily, the Holy Spirit began to speak to me.

I honestly don't remember what Fr. John said but it was one of those times that I've heard priests talk about. They say that people come up to them and say thank you for saying such and such and they didn't even say what the person thought they heard. I think this was what happened to me. Whatever he said allowed me to hear an interior voice.

The Lord said to me: "Debbie you have been very generous with your time and talent, but you have been stingy with your money when it comes to tithing." My heart was immediately saddened. There is no part of me that wants to hurt my Lord. As I sat there searching my thoughts, I knew there was some truth to this. You see, like many of us, I felt that I was the exception to the rule regarding God's directive on tithing. I was being very generous with my time and talent but my faith was not strong enough to obey God's directives. I was sure that what I gave in time and talent would balance the scales. We have always given monetarily, but never a full 10 percent.

I went home and told Kenny what I had heard. I explained to him that I was convicted that we must begin to tithe a full 10 percent. After all, 10 percent of a little isn't that much. We figured what could it hurt? We were at the end of our credit, and it was looking like we weren't going to be able to make the next month's house payment. Understand that we didn't act upon this as a last ditch effort. It was truly out of obedience and desire to please God. Our Lord didn't really want our money, what He wanted was us to trust and obey Him.

The next day, I went to confession before Mass. I told Fr. John all that I had heard the day before. I wanted to start clean in other areas that we had not been obedient as well as confess a true sorrow for our lack of trust for Papa to provide for our financial needs. He said Debbie, you know what it says in *Malachi 3:10-12. Bring the full tithes into the storehouse, that there may be food in my house; and thereby put me to the test, says the Lord of hosts, if I will not open the windows of heaven for you and pour down for you an overflowing blessing. 11 I will rebuke the devourer for you, so that it will not destroy the fruits of your soil; and your vine in the field shall not fail to bear, says the Lord of hosts. 12 Then all nations will call you blessed, for you will be a land of delight, says the Lord of hosts.*

He then said, "Why don't you put the Lord to the test? You see, I've come to know that all of His word is true or none of it is!"

The grace that I received that day in the sacrament of reconciliation was phenomenal. Sunday morning came and I got the calculator out and figured out what ten percent of my earnings were. It was amazing that I was able to write the check effortlessly. Let me say that we started giving the full 10 percent to the church. In our diocese it is recommended to give 5 percent to your church and the other 5 percent to a charity of your choice. We wanted to be sure that we gave the full amount in the beginning to the church. It felt wonderful to put that check in the basket.

All the while this crisis was happening, Kenny was looking for other means of employment. At age 60 with no experience with technology, he seemed to always run into a brick wall. No one wanted to hire him. He was driving a 1994 pickup truck with 260,000 miles on it. We called his truck Sandy Brown. Sandy was a work horse but he didn't have reverse, so Kenny had to think about where he parked so as to not be stuck without reverse. Sandy Brown was dented but we were thankful for even having a truck.

As I am relaying this story, I am being brought to a deeper level of love for my husband. This took humility to drive an old vehicle like that, but that's Kenny. He always put our family's needs before his own. As for the salon, I worked very hard. This did create quite a bit of pressure on me, but I was keeping my eyes on the plow and not looking back. In times past, I was super-focused on how much money I could make in a day. Now, since I purely saw my workplace as a ministry, I simply would walk in the door and say: "Give us this day our daily bread." I knew God knew what we needed that day to pay the bills. It was amazing that most days it would be just a few dollars more than what we needed.

After we began tithing a full 10 percent, my prayer began to go something like this. "Lord, we are doing as you have asked concerning our tithing, this is your problem now." Maybe this was a bit bold, but I really believed His word. God is never early or late, but always on time. My peace was still present but my heart was breaking. I'll have to admit that I was a bit bitter that everything we had worked for all these years seemed to be slipping away. Our future was on sinking sand. This is not what I thought my life would be like at this point in time. It took everything in me to surrender to the will of God. If this was our fate, we would start all over like we had 44 years earlier. After all, we had our faith in God, our family was intact, and we were still in love and healthy. Did anything else really matter?

It was only about a month after we had started tithing that one of my salesmen came into the salon with a new type of curling machine. You won't believe what it was called. It was called a "Miracurl." I should have known God was up to something with a name like that!

These handy little curling machines retailed for $225, which is quite a hefty ticket item, but they looked unique so I thought I would invest in a couple to see how they would sell. As soon as they came in, they sold. I ordered again, only doubled my order. They were gone again in a flash. I started ordering 10-15 at a time and I couldn't keep them in stock. My profit range on these curling machines was very good. I was watching the "Miracurl" bring a miracle to our finances.

I was told by my salesman that I sold more of these curling machines that summer than anyone else in the country. The boost that this gave us financially kept us going through the summer. In about another month, we got a check in the mail for $1,500. Somehow we were involved in a class action lawsuit settlement and this was due us. The next week we got a check in the mail for overpayment in our escrow account. It was around $500. I was doing the happy dance because this bought us a bit more time. My friend, who I mentioned earlier, gave us another large check.

Was God really beginning to move on our part? Were we coming out on the other side of this very long Via Dolorosa?

And then it happened. I got a call from Kenny while I was at work. It was in the middle of the afternoon and I stepped outside to take it. I couldn't believe what I was hearing on the other end. He told me that the department head of the city building and code enforcement had called him to see if he was interested in coming to work for the city as a building inspector. I thought that I was going to faint! I couldn't believe my ears. I kept saying I can't believe this. This is a miracle. Then I said, "You did tell him yes, didn't you?"

He had a 9:00 a.m. meeting with him the next day and by 9:15 he had the job. God not only delivered us but brought Kenny a job that used the skills he had honed over many years. We had no idea that this job was even posted and, even if we had, he might not have applied because of the computer skills the job required. He was very open about his lack of technology and his boss said it didn't matter. It was the first time in our 40 years of marriage that we would have great health benefits, vision and dental insurance, and even a truck and phone for him to use. The benefits plus the salary and we were in the tomb awaiting resurrection day!

Five years have passed since that day. While we are still trying to dig out, God did as He said He would. My friends, Fr. John and Fr. Mark were very happy for us.

Now, the Lord loves us to give testimony for the good He has done, but this was such a private matter, and I didn't want to cause any shame or embarrassment to Kenny, so I only shared privately as I felt the Lord asked me to. You see, the enemy was still trying to put that shame on us. He surely didn't want us to speak out about the Lord's generosity.

The story doesn't end here. Our pastor called me one day only a few months later to see if we would share our story at all the weekend Masses for our tithing campaign. I told him that I certainly had no problem with it, but it would be Kenny's decision. If we agreed, our story would be heard publicly by more than 6,000 people. This truly called for a total surrender of our pride.

Have you ever been asked to share publicly something very personal such as this? Is the enemy trying to cover you in shame?

All I can say is that Kenny agreed and we did give our testimony. It was awesome to give praise to our Lord for what He had done for us. After we spoke, we had many people thank us for being so transparent. Our hope is that our story gave glory to God.

Loving trust means an absolute, unconditional,
and unwavering confidence in God
our loving Father, even when everything seems to be a
total failure;
to look to him alone as our help and protector,
trusting to the point of rashness
with courageous confidence in his fatherly goodness

—St. Mother Theresa

CHAPTER 11

BREAKING FREE

I s there something in your life that has a strong hold on you, something that besets your soul? What is it that you are addicted to? Yes, I know that you're thinking that you really aren't addicted to anything, but in reading Richard Rohr's book *Breathing Underwater*, I came to understand that any area of our lives where we have the propensity to sin is an addiction to some disordered desire.

Addictions come in all sorts of flavors. Food, drugs, sex, busyness, laziness, pornography, social media, nicotine, pride (the ego or false self), or even religion itself can all become addictions. Yes, I said religion because we can become addicted to trying to follow the rules to the point that we lose the spirit of the law and begin to follow the letter of the law. We somehow reach a mindset that we can become holy by doing good as if it depended on our own doing. Holiness is all given freely through the commodity of grace.

Life can and should be a constant desire to break free of those things that weigh us down. These are the things that keep us out of order spiritually. Every time we reach for one of these disordered desires, we are choosing, not just to sin, but to remain in bondage and separate from God. It's like hanging an out-of-order sign on us that reads: "I'm not working right today."

There is good news, however, stated in **Romans 5:20 *Law came in, to increase the trespass; but where sin increased, grace abounded all the more.***

The law is to show us that without grace we cannot get it right on our own! Paul states this in another way: *I do not understand my own actions. For I do not do what I want, but I do the very thing I hate.* - **Romans 7:15**

MANY YEARS AGO, while in high school, one of my friends asked me if I wanted a cigarette. I really didn't want it, but like most young people, I was easily influenced by my peers for both good and bad. I remember not even liking or enjoying the experience. That should have been enough to stop me, but it didn't. I kept thinking that maybe I would learn to like the taste and smell. What I did like, was the feeling of being "a part of" or "the same as." I remember thinking that I was being disobedient, but that I was old enough to choose for myself what I wanted.

This decision-making process was disordered. Now, some 45 years later, I know that the question I should have asked is: "Will this decision bring me closer to Christ?" Whatever the decision is that we are making we should always ask ourselves "How will this bring me closer to Christ? Will this choice hinder my relationship with the Lord?"

The choice to smoke cigarettes, to be disobedient to the rules of my home, opened the door for many more choices to defy the ground rules that were set for me. Next came alcohol, and then curfews and before I knew it, I was heading down a slippery slope. It is by the grace of God that some of the choices I made didn't end up any worse. I know that it was my mama and daddy's prayers that probably kept me safe. I was never the child that didn't take into consideration how my poor choices would hurt my parents. Nevertheless, letting down my guard so many years ago, brought about a struggle that I carried into more recent years, which is what I want to convey to you now.

Addiction in any form will cause a person to choose the addiction over family, friends or even God. People who are addicted will lie, steal, cheat, con or do just about anything to get what they want. While many of you may think that cigarettes are hardly an addiction, for me they were. I kept hearing that my body was a temple of the Holy Spirit. If that is so, and it is, I knew that I was playing with fire in my temple. My choice of smoking could bring harm to my physical body. My body, your body, is sacred. I didn't want to cause sickness, yet I kept buying cigarettes.

Something that I heard a preacher say one day is that sin will take you where you don't want to go, keep you longer than you want to stay, and cost you more than you want to pay! Can you relate? The enemy will lure you to make sinful choices and then he will heap such a shame and guilt on you for your choices that it can destroy all of your peace. This is how choosing to smoke up my temple affected me.

What really bothered me the most was that I was lying to my husband and daughter about smoking. How foolish could I be? They knew I was smoking, but the shame of doing it made me lie. I went through more perfume that anyone could imagine. I didn't want to be a poor influence on anyone, yet I kept on smoking. At this point I had stopped and started smoking many times over the years. I really don't know what made me snap the last time, since I had been off cigarettes for nearly 20 years.

What does this tell you and me? I believe the phrase "If not for the grace of God go I." Anyone can fall at any time. Anyone can relapse at any time. I know this to be truth for sure. How did I overcome this time? The verse I mentioned in Romans 5 earlier resurfaced with power again. If sin was present, so much more was grace. I knew that I must exchange something good for my habit if I wanted to quit. I knew that I needed God's help. I knew that I was too weak to do this on my own so I asked God for the grace to stop and what I replaced smoking with was daily Mass attendance.

At first it was hard getting up so early to attend Mass. Three mornings a week Mass was at 7 a.m. and two days a week it was at 6 p.m. But with God's grace, I was determined. The more I went, the easier it became. The easier it became, the more I received. Little did I know that God was going to use this one stumbling block of smoking and turn it into something very powerful.

Romans 8:28 is a promise that God can bring good from bad: *We know that in everything God works for good with those who love him, who are called according to his purpose.*

SOMEWHERE DURING THIS DAILY Mass journey, and I'm pretty sure it was early on, I had a succession of blows hit me that were heartbreaking. I had two employees leave at the same time, and I had a personal issue with a close friend that blew up to epic proportions. The business side wasn't a new thing to me, but the friend issue was something I had never gone through before. I felt my friend and I were very close and the issue stretched into other areas with other friends. I was heartbroken about it all. I'm sure that my friend was wounded in all of this as well. I tried to talk to her but she shut down. I tried to write but the reply was to leave her alone. I felt betrayed and I know she did as well. Once again God turned this into Romans 8:28 situation. What does all this have to do with breaking free? Keep reading and you will see!

Day in and day out I went to Mass. I would sit there and cry most of the time. Each day the Lord did not disappoint. He touched me deeply each day through the scripture read at Mass, the homilies, or just the peaceful presence of the Holy Spirit. I also frequented the sacrament of reconciliation. The Lord began to speak very clearly to my heart. He told me one day that He knew what betrayal felt like. He told me that if I wanted to be like him I had to learn to bear the same wounds. What I didn't recognize right in the beginning of all this was that the Lord was helping me break free from the addiction of human opinion and esteem. He was helping me be stripped of my false self and get to the core of my true identity.

The place where my true value and worth is just being a child of God. I realized that it did bother me what others thought of me and that all that really mattered is how God sees me.

It was a beautiful fall night in October 2010, October 22 to be exact. Kenny and I were sitting outside on our deck just talking and enjoying a glass of wine together. The sky was exceptionally beautiful because there was an awesome full Hunter's moon to enjoy. With only a few clouds here and there, the night sky was illuminating the ground and my aching heart. It is times like this that the images transported me back to the peaceful country Camelot life I had as a young girl. It was a carefree time and life was simple. I was protected from many of the harmful things that getting older brings.

Now the way I process things is to talk them over and over. Poor Kenny was trying his best to listen, but I know it is hard on him at times. This was one of those nights that I sat there and poured my heart out to him and to God. I didn't understand why this had happened to me. There are painful details of this story that I have left out intentionally because they really don't matter much. What is important is that when we cry out to God He really listens and sometimes he answers us in such a way that we are spellbound. His phone number is **Jeremiah 33:3 - *Call to me and I will answer you, and will tell you great and hidden things which you have not known.***

Kenny had listened intently for quite a while when he said that he wanted to go back in the house. I was fine with that, but I wasn't finished talking to God. Once again the moon and the stars made me feel the presence of God. I was so inspired that I went in the house to get my camera to take pictures of the moon and the sky. I'm not a photographer. In fact, the camera I was using was just a simple camera I had borrowed to take pictures of my daughter Abbey since she was on her college homecoming court at the University of Central Arkansas. I snapped away with tears in my eyes and a sense of peace and joy in my heart. I wanted some pictures of this beautiful moon.

Now, I didn't have any idea what the camera captured because it wasn't the type that allowed you to see the pictures right after you took them. With some sense of peace and closure in my heart, I went inside and tried to release mercy and forgiveness into my spirit. I laid the camera down and forgot about it for almost a week.

With thoughts of the celebration of Abbey on homecoming court, I was inspired to take the sim card to get the pictures developed. I had never used a kiosk before to develop prints. As the kind young man behind the counter was walking me through the pictures I came upon the pictures of the full moon I had taken the week before. I had actually forgotten about taking them. Frame by frame I looked at each picture smiling at the beauty and joy of my daughter and then I couldn't believe what I was seeing and neither could the young man. He asked me what is that on that picture?

I told him it was supposed to be a picture of the full moon like the rest, but on this one, the moon was in the shape of a cross. That's what it looked like to me. When I took the pictures, all I saw in the lens of the camera was a round ball in the sky. What came out on this particular shot was amazing. You have to see this picture because you would never believe it if you did not lay eyes on the picture itself. There was nothing done to this picture; no photoshopping it in any way. As I looked at it I heard the words *"teaching them to observe all that I have commanded you; and lo, I am with you always, to the close of the age."* - **Matthew 28:20**

No matter the circumstances, God is faithful to us. He will never leave us or forsake us. I feel like God has given me the most precious gift every time I look at this picture. Not only does it bless me, but I have told the story over and over in my salon as my clients sit in my chair. I have it framed on my work station and I just wait for people to ask me about it. As I have shared this story, there have been many reactions. Some have cried, some have received great delight. I am sure that there are some who don't know me very well that raise an eyebrow with doubt; but it is what it is and only God could strike this image. Now as I said before, many see a cross, but some have seen an angel. With eyes of faith, the spiritual realm is brought a bit closer to us. Angels do serve God and they are also there to help us. I have given this picture away to hundreds of people. As you look at it, I hope God speaks to your heart as he has so many others.

What I'm trying to convey here is that an addiction, as bad as it is, can be used as a gift to help us grow. If I hadn't been smoking, I might not have made the decision to try to overcome the habit by attending Mass daily. The graces I have been given at daily Mass are immense. Each day the Lord dealt with me gently as He helped me to see my true self. The addiction of my ego needing to be lifted up was dealt with right at that altar each day.

My ego wasn't the only thing that was dealt with at daily Mass. It was at daily Mass that I received the graces necessary to make it through the financial crisis that beset us. My addiction to be in control of my finances came into sharp focus. It was at daily Mass that I walked with Jesus through the pain of sickness in my family.

Daily Mass gave me the grace to discern how my business needed to evolve and change. Daily Mass was where I learned to hear the Lord more clearly. It was at daily Mass that I fell deeper and deeper in love with the Father, Son, Holy Spirit and our Queen Mother Mary. It was at daily Mass that my eyes were opened in the breaking of the bread. It was at daily Mass that I was corrected when in the wrong. It was at daily Mass that I was given the encouragement to keep moving forward to become a spiritual director. You might think that smoking isn't too bad of an addiction, but for me it was. I have others as well.

I believe that most of us want to bury our mistakes. It is true that we shouldn't let them keep us beat down, but it is also true that our brokenness can be a beautiful gift when it has been redeemed by the blood of Christ. Our brokenness is something beautiful and valuable to our life journey. Maybe you have seen the saying: "Here in the South, we don't hide crazy, we just put it on the front porch and give it a sweet tea." Transparency allows others to approach you when they are in similar circumstances. Put your crazy on your front porch and let it be a reminder of how the grace of God has changed you, use it for the glory of God, and then drink a little tea in celebration!

Breaking free has many facets. I want to give a few more examples of how the Lord is freeing me from disordered desires or disordered thinking. The financial crisis that we went through was one that God used to show me not only my desire to be in control of my finances but also how much it bothered me to think that others knew the mess we were in. EGO! All the different situations that I have gone through over the years like owning my own business have shown me where I was wrong as an employer (humility), as well as how to see Christ in each person that sits in my chair. We are not all the same and that's a good thing. God creates each of us uniquely. It is arrogant to think that everyone should be like you.

What are the desires of your heart? What might be some areas that could block those deep longings? Are your desires in right order?

You heard about our oldest son and his wife having fertility issues. Would you believe that my younger son and his wife Meridee had a fertility issue as well? I was talking with the Lord and I said: "Are you serious? Not again? What is the deal here, Lord?" Once again, we started praying for a baby. Maybe this is my specialty. Who knows?

So Anthony and Meridee began the journey that sometimes is a long road to discern what might be causing their situation of infertility. I can only imagine what this is like. I do know, as a woman, how strong the desire to have a baby was for me. Lots of decisions, along with lots of doctors' visits, along with much prayer and tears is the journey of infertility and, if you're Catholic, there's the whole issue of what's permitted in the tenets of our faith.

I could feel fear and anxiety starting to creep into my mind. I wanted a baby for them as much as I wanted life for myself. As I was praying about the why's of the infertility and babies out of wedlock in my family, I **thought** that the Lord spoke to me about it. Now, I'm not talking about an audible voice, but an interior knowing that you've read about in previous chapters. **Whenever you think something is of God you must always test the spirits.**

I was brought back to my younger years. I thought about the times I had practiced birth control through the use of the pill. I was reminded of other areas where I had not been chaste before marriage. Were the sins of the father and mother resting on my children? And what does that mean anyway? Did my past have something to do with the generations after me? Did I somehow contribute to this infertility issue? I was starting to feel shame, which is not how God works. It took some prayer and some silence as I listened to the Lord. I even sought answers from my Spiritual Director. Why would God punish the generations after me for my sinful behavior? As I stayed with this I began to see that my image of God needed to be refocused. Some of my old learned images of God as the God who was waiting to get us if we messed up had crept in.

You've heard people say if God is good, why does he let bad things happen? Where is God during great suffering? As my spiritual director says: "God is in the answer!" He shows up when people come together after the disasters. He comes when someone comforts the infertile woman. God is the face of Jesus and we know Jesus' main message was healing, love and mercy. Not pointing fingers, not punishing the innocent. Were these thoughts from the Lord or from the enemy trying to bring shame into an area that had already been confessed? Who was talking to me?

This whole infertility issue caused me to go deeper into my own past and ask why did I do these things? What area was I bound up in that caused this behavior? If we don't address the bindings, they will still keep us hostage and we'll probably keep shame, fear or bondage as our friends. This example is to make you aware of the tactics of the enemy. He loves to bring doubt, shame, lies and anything else he can throw at you to cause you to believe him and not God's word.

The truth is that because of our fallen nature, sickness entered into all of our lives. Maybe the issues they experienced with infertility was just how life was playing out for them. *As he passed by, he saw a man blind from his birth. 2 And his disciples asked him, "Rabbi, who sinned, this man or his parents, that he was born blind?" 3 Jesus answered, "It was not that this man sinned, or his parents, but that the works of God might be made manifest in him. - John 9:1-3*

So now let me share how the power of God can be seen in this story! Don't you want to hear the whole pregnancy story? I sure want to tell you. Again, as I share this story, this is how it related to me. I think that you might be surprised and even chuckle a bit when you see my faith and my craziness! Even the best intentioned followers of Jesus have their places of testing. Remember in the South we don't hide our crazy!

Anthony and Meridee had been married several years when they discerned they were ready for a baby. After realizing there could be a problem, Meridee, who had been seeing a doctor regularly, decided that it was time to seek help from a specialist.

Around this same time period, Meridee decided that she wanted to enter into the Catholic Church. It was something that she fully decided to do on her own and she asked me to be her sponsor. I was honored beyond words. Each week we discussed the faith and, in the car rides to and from church, we also discussed different issues as they were presenting themselves with the baby process. Now as I mentioned before, we don't always know for sure if what we are hearing is from God, but I felt like this time it was. I knew the healing power of the Eucharist and I felt that once Meridee was able to receive Jesus in the Holy Sacrament, she would get pregnant.

There was also another thing that I got into my head about this whole baby process. Each of my children received a Nativity set from Kenny and me when they got married. I noticed the first year I gave it to them, it wasn't out. The next year, Anthony told me that the set that I gave them was missing the baby Jesus. I couldn't believe it. I also got in my head that their house needed a baby Jesus as a sign of hope that with God all things are possible. Somehow I thought this was part of the fertility journey.

Now this was the Christmas before Meridee entered the church. So it's the week of Christmas, and I am driven to find a baby Jesus that would be just the right size for their creche. Do you know how hard this is? I went from store to store looking for baby Jesus. I just couldn't seem to find the right one until I entered a hardware store near me. There He was! The perfect size, but it was the whole set. I didn't have the money to spend to buy the whole set so I stood there and began to devise a plan. I was a woman on a mission. I had to get baby Jesus in their home. I would do anything to help this baby to be conceived. Now here's where I started going south and how my plan was not in line with Jesus'. Notice I said *I* would do anything. . . I, I, I.

As I stood there, this thought ran through my head. I could just take (cough cough), well, really steal is the better word, that baby Jesus. After all, my set didn't have one when I bought it. It was only right that I take this one. I was entitled. Enter disordered desire. As I stood there thinking about how this would play out, I began to come to my senses. Somehow, it just seemed a bit wrong that I was contemplating how to steal Jesus. I could see the local newspaper headlines: "Local hairdresser caught red-handed stealing baby Jesus." Quickly I came to my senses and left the store.

I prayed this time and said: "Lord where can a woman find a baby Jesus in this town?" I chuckled a bit when I immediately heard "Go to Walmart," and so I did. There He was, one lonely baby Jesus just waiting for me to buy him at the high price of 99 cents. I was a happy lady and thankfully, I didn't end up stealing Jesus. I wrapped Him up with the scripture verses: *And Mary said to the angel, "How shall this be, since I have no husband?" 35 And the angel said to her, "The Holy Spirit will come upon you, and the power of the Most High will overshadow you; therefore the child to be born will be called holy, the Son of God. 36 And behold, your kinswoman Elizabeth in her old age has also conceived a son; and this is the sixth month with her who was called barren. 37 For with God nothing will be impossible." Luke 1:34-37*

My faith was back in right order thinking and all was well. Jesus was in the house.

So it's the first of the New Year and we're on our way to RCIA classes and getting one step closer to Meridee entering the church. RCIA stands for the Rite of Christian Initiation for adults. As we were driving, I asked Meridee what confirmation name she had chosen. She told me St. Gianna Molla. I smiled because in my heart I knew some about this saint. She was a Catholic doctor who, while pregnant, had chosen the life of her child over her own life. I felt like this was a beautiful saint for Meridee. I've heard it said that we don't choose the saints they choose us and I think St. Gianna did just that!

That night while I was driving back to my house, the Lord and I had a conversation. I talk to Him just like I talk to anybody else. Here's how the conversation went. "Lord, if I were you, I think I would let Meridee get pregnant on St. Gianna's feast day. It would be a great way to teach her about the power of the saints and their prayers for us." When I got home, I looked up her feast day. To my surprise, it was right after Easter that year on April 28. I was so excited because Meridee would be receiving Jesus in the Eucharist regularly by then and then St. Gianna would be praying for her as well.

Without giving you all the details, Meridee and Anthony conceived their first child on this doctor saint's feast day! It was no coincidence that St. Gianna was a doctor and a mother who valued life. She picked Meridee and I'm so glad. For Meridee's pushing gift in child labor, Anthony gave Meridee a St. Gianna medal. You've gotten a very condensed version of a journey that our family went on, but especially as it related to Meridee and Anthony's experience. Saylor, our beautiful four-year-old girl now has a precious baby brother who is nearing his second birthday. I'm so proud of this beautiful couple as they live out a faith-filled life!

God has been good to me, despite my trying to get in the way. Even when my thoughts might get a bit disordered, His grace brings me back to true north.

This year during the Christmas season, I received many gifts. I loved them all, however, a couple that I received from the Lord were probably the most beneficial to me. After opening these gifts you are about to hear about, I realize they all contained the same thing. Humility. . . . Whenever a gift is given, it is good to take time to look at it, savor it, and then enjoy it.

In the 62 years I've been on planet earth, I don't believe that I've ever attended Christmas Mass alone – until 2017. Due to injury, and family situations, I set out for our Christmas Eve services alone. It felt so strange to me.

As I got closer and closer to church, lots of thoughts and emotions were running through my head. Who would I sit by? I can't believe I'm going alone. Poor Debbie! What will everyone think when they see me by myself? Reflecting back on all of this, I can see clearly one big problem. It was all about me! My ego and pride were in full operational mode! I scanned the church as I looked for a place to sit. I realized that I better just take a seat before there wasn't one left. There was no time to be picky!

Consequently, I sat by total strangers on one side, but on the other side of me were friends that I had gotten to know through daily Mass. I was so happy to be with my "church family." Our church is a large congregation, so it's easy to be around people you haven't met. Thoughts raced through my mind. Will Tina and Dutch wonder why I am alone? Do these people I don't know, realize I have a very large family? Will they be friendly to me? Oh, poor me! I surveyed all the large families who had gathered to celebrate with each other. I thought of all the years in the past that I had all of my family with me. I had become quite proud of the fact that we had grown large enough to take a full row, and were needing to start filling another pew.

I don't want you to get the idea that I was there for just the show. I did try very hard to stay focused on the reason for the season, but at that time in my life, I was too busy looking at my family and everybody else's to stay connected to that wonderful gift of the newborn king. After trying to talk myself into a stupor, I decided to focus on the real reason I was at this beautiful liturgy.

I stilled my soul and began to adore Jesus. I knew that I could either feel sorry for myself or I could enter into real worship. I chose to enter into the Holy of Holies. As I worshiped Jesus, he began to speak to my heart. Understand when I say that he was speaking to me, this is an interior knowing that I've become familiar with and I knew this was His voice because it was a gentle, teaching voice.

Sometimes he speaks to me with visions and words. I began to see myself in the pew with all my family. I was happy and very proud. Now that is not a bad way to think of your family, but there was a teaching here for me. I began to hear the Lord say that the pride I had for my family when I want everyone to see them with me in church, wasn't in good order. I wanted everyone to see that my family is good. My family is loyal; and they are that for sure, but they were not trophies to be paraded around in church for everyone to see. My pride at those times was not in right order. My family was not for show, but for love and service.

They are gifts from God to Kenny and me and it really doesn't matter what anyone else thinks about them or our family as a whole. I don't want to make you think that I don't love my family fiercely because I do and I don't use them, but at times I think that I want everyone to think that my tribe is perfect. That is where the problem lies. We are not perfect, we are perfectly flawed; but we are also works in progress and God loves each of us very much just the way we are.

It never occurred to me how the parading of my family might make someone else feel. The Holy Spirit began to make me see the couples who never had children, the single people who longed for family, the aged whose family is never with them at church. The very lonely people who just want someone to say hi or invite them for coffee. Instead of trying to show them off, I should have been more humble. I should have just thanked God the whole time for the beautiful gift they are to Kenny and me. I should have been thanking God for the grace we received in raising them and how they turned out to be good Christian people raising great

Christian families. I should have been adoring the Lord more and focusing on them less while in church.

The second gift that came right around the "Epiphany" was exposure of the jealously that can harbor in my heart. Yuck. . . . yeah this is the part we don't want others to see; those parts that are present in every human but that are disordered and have to be brought before the Lord to allow our spirits to become freer each day.

I love to serve the Lord in varied ways and I especially like the challenge of new opportunities to do that. A very close friend, that I truly love as a sister, was who God chose to teach me this lesson. My friend Diane and I do so many spiritual things together. We are like honeysuckle vines that have been planted side by side, working together to give off a beautiful fragrance to the Lord. Our lives have been intertwined with each other for about 45 years. We've worked tirelessly together in the kingdom of God for most of these 45 years.

I was having a pretty good day when something that Diane told me, changed the tone. Like I mentioned, we've done most ministries together so when Diane told me that she had been asked to be a director for a silent retreat, I was just a bit surprised. This would be the first time for her to do this and I have had not yet had this opportunity. It's something that I really want to do and I suppose I just figured we would do that together the first time. I was happy for her but very quickly I felt a bit of jealousy take root in my heart. Believe me, she is very qualified to do this. I don't know why I couldn't just be happy for her. Instead of feeling pure joy for her, I allowed the enemy to get a foothold and create sadness and jealousy, then shame entered in for feeling this way. As quick as that entered my heart, I knew it was wrong.

I knew that this had to go straight to the confessional on the very same day. As I stood in line for my turn, tears were filling my eyes. I was truly sorry for having offended God. Once again, the

Lord began to speak to me. I got the feeling that I was acting like a spoiled brat. I was being jealous of my sister for something she deserved. My Papa wanted to give her something and I was jealous and competitive with my sister.

I began to think of my own children. Now my two boys love each other fiercely, but they can get into some jousting/teasing matches at times on what they have or what they are doing. I began to think how I would feel if they were jealous of each other. It would break my heart. I love them both so very much and I want them both to know that I am proud of each of them for what they have been able to accomplish. I want them both to know that I see their unique goodness and that they each are living out their lives in unique ways. As I imagined how I would feel if this were to happen in my family, I began to weep. I knew that this was exactly how I was acting and that I was hurting my Papa!

When I sat down face-to-face with Fr. Tony in the confessional, the sorrow was almost unbearable; not only for what I had done but for the insight of how we hurt our Father in heaven when we are sinful. That's our daddy and we are breaking His heart when we act this way.

Actually when you have the humility to confess these imperfections, and a good confessor, they can become great graces in our life. I will have a completely new attitude now each time a sin besets me. Fr. Tony also helped to see how I could take the disappointment I was feeling for not getting picked and turn it into a prayer for my friend and another one of my Spiritual Direction classmates who was working the same retreat weekend. He described it like me being able to be in two places at once. I could offer my pain as prayer for them in another city and I could still go about my own ministry right where I was! This brought joy to me and a fresh perspective again on how my sin can actually bring me closer to the Lord if I am humble enough to admit my faults.

At the same time I was processing these movements in my heart, I was doing an in-home Retreat in Daily Life. This is for people who would like to do a 30-day silent retreat, but due to their state in life, are unable to leave home that long. At one point in the process you make an election for your state in life. It's something that I wanted to take very seriously and enter into with all my heart. Many scriptures and thoughts had been brought to me in prayer by this time in the retreat. One of the readings/meditations was the three degrees of humility. The Lord was obviously not finished teaching me all the he wanted me to know about humility and fear. The three degrees of humility are:

1. Humility for the Sake of Salvation. This is the base line minimum humility. It is necessary to turn away from the seductive power of sin and toward a life following God.

> "I would want to do nothing that would cut me from God—not even were I made head of all creation or even just to save my own life here on earth. I know that grave sin in this sense is to miss the whole meaning of being a person—one who is created and redeemed and is destined to live forever in love with God my Creator and Lord" (Fleming #165).

Even though the first degree is the "base line" level, gradual conversion to this first degree is just as much a cause of rejoicing as conversion to any of the other degrees. So many people in our world (myself included) too often forget the richness of God's love, the purity of his call, and the power of his mercy and grace. When we accept those realities over our sinfulness, we enter into the first degree. There is nothing easy about this step, so when it happens, let us praise God and rejoice with others.

2. Humility for a Detached Life. The second degree calls us to a freedom from our preferences, habits, and anything else that we

consider to be ours so that we may more readily follow Christ just as Christ followed the will of God the Father above all else.

> "My life is firmly grounded in the fact that the reality of being a person is seen fully in Jesus Christ. . . . With this habitual attitude, I find that I can maintain a certain balance in my inclinations to have riches rather than poverty, honor rather than dishonor, or to desire a long life rather than a short life" (Fleming, #166).

In this step a person begins to see just how large the mission of bringing about the Kingdom of God really is. The Kingdom of God is not this world's utopia, but rather, something of Heaven. As such, some of the commonly accepted ways of the world (e.g., honors, riches, security) are not always beneficial but distracting to the Kingdom of God. The second degree of humility opens our minds to that reality and frees our behavior so that it can choose whatever will best lead our Christian community more closely to the commands of Christ. To do the humble things that need to be done, but that no one else wants to do, is a tall order. Thus, like with the first degree, we should rejoice and praise God when we see models of the second degree of humility.

3. Humility for Love of the Poor Christ. The final and most pure degree of humility, the third degree, propels us to live a very humble style of life similar to Christ's life for no other reason than a sincere and profound love for the poor Christ. Rather than concerning itself first with one's own well-being or with doing the right thing, this degree is centered around nothing more than pure love for Jesus.

> "I so much want the truth of Christ's life to be fully the truth of my own that I find myself, moved by grace, with a love and a desire for poverty in order to be with the poor

Christ; a love and a desire for insults in order to be closer to Christ in his own rejection by people; a love and a desire to be considered worthless and a fool for Christ, rather than be esteemed as wise and prudent according to the standards of the world" (Fleming #167).

Names come to mind of people like St. Paul, St. Joan of Arc, The Ugandan Martyrs, Blessed Miguel Pro, Walter Ciszek, Dorothy Day, and Martin Luther King Jr. This degree of humility is prophetic. It captures our imaginations and confounds our minds. It is at one and the same time painful and beautiful just as Christ's life was both painful and beautiful. http://www.magisspirituality.org/spex_reflection/1-2-3-degrees-of-humility/

As I read these three degrees of humility, I felt I could say yes to the first two degrees, but the last one. . . It was tough. Could I choose poverty over wealth, could I say yes to be ridiculed like Christ, to be despised and rejected for the sake of Christ? Could I be all-in 100 percent for the Lord?

I thought I had already reached this level of surrender but the Lord was showing me differently. There was some fear that was holding me back. I had to pray more on this third degree of humility. Why was I afraid? I left my house that morning headed to spiritual direction. As I was praying about this degree of humility and what I would bring to direction, a car passed me on the interstate. On the rear window were the words: BE HUMBLE. I couldn't believe what I was seeing. I actually laughed out loud.

I shared all of this with my spiritual director and he asked me to look into the reasons I was having a hard time to commit. As I prayed throughout the day, I realized it was fear keeping me from saying yes fully. The next morning when I woke up, I was getting dressed with this still on my mind and a grace came over me that actually was profound yet simple. As I thought on this, I realized that God is sovereign over my life completely. Why was I wrestling with Him? Did I really believe that He was for my good and not disaster? If God brought something my way, wasn't it for the well-being of my soul as well as others. It seemed almost ridiculous that I was resisting God. If He wanted me to be ridiculed, then so be it. If he wanted me to be poor, then, that was for His glory and for His kingdom. I could see that fear was holding me back and also a lack of trust. I heard the words: ***What then shall we say to this? If God is for us, who is against us?*** - **Romans 8:31.** As I was present to God in that moment, I said my yes. My soul was at peace.

ANOTHER AREA that I really needed to be set free was from the fear of getting dementia when I am older. This disease has infested my mother's side of the family and, if you remember from earlier chapters, it stole my mother's last fourteen years of life. When you are fairly young and you watch this thieving disease take your loved one, you can't help but get anxious. The problem for me was that it scared me to death and the fear of it festered in my mind for many years. Most of our battles are fought in our minds. This is a place where the enemy can sure get a foothold if you let him. I am sad to say, I managed to let him take root in my mind and let fear settle in.

I had to address the fear or it would have ruined my day-to-day living. It took lots of prayer and some intense spiritual direction sessions but one day, by the grace of God, I finally got everything in perspective. Most fear is rooted in the lack of trust. The bottom line is that I knew that no matter what happened to me, God would be with me. I had to trust the fact that my children would do their best for me. How that might play out I couldn't control. I couldn't control it any more than I could control my mother's situation. My disordered desire was to be in control. What I have control over is thanking God every day for my sound mind, living a healthy life, praying healing verses over my body, and leaving the outcome to God!

Do you have fear? What are some of your disordered desires? What is it that is stealing your joy? What has a stronghold on you? Are you afraid to say yes to God fully? Know who and what you are fighting. Satan is your enemy and he uses the strongholds to tear you down. Call upon the Holy Spirit and walk in that power. Begin to see the battle won and don't cower to the enemy.

One thing that you can do is to take authority over the situations with the power of the Holy Spirit. Jesus has already won the battle for you; you must claim it. Believe the word of God and enter into the heavenly realm of revelation truth. Don't just read the Bible, let it reveal God's truth to you and transform you. That's what happened to me when I went to daily Mass. Ask for the Holy Spirit to open your eyes and heart in a fresh way. Speak blessings and not curses on yourself.

Luke 6:45 says: *The good man out of the good treasure of his heart produces good, and the evil man out of his evil treasure produces evil; for out of the abundance of the heart his mouth speaks.*

What is in your heart? Fear or the power of the living God? Decree and declare what is rightfully yours. Reject the negativity and replace it with God's words. Surround yourself with Christian friends that are living in the revelation truth. Pray daily and don't try to win the battle alone. You need the Holy Spirit. If you haven't made a born again profession of faith, ask for the Holy Spirit to take authority over your life. Get up every day and put on the armor of God.

Ephesians 6:10-18 - *10 Finally, be strong in the Lord and in the strength of his might. 11 Put on the whole armor of God, that you may be able to stand against the wiles of the devil. 12 For we are not contending against flesh and blood, but against the principalities, against the powers, against the world rulers of this present darkness, against the* *spiritual hosts of wickedness in the heavenly places. 13 Therefore take the whole armor of God, that you may be able to withstand in the evil day, and having done all, to stand. 14 Stand therefore, having girded your loins with truth, and having put on the breastplate of righteous-ness, 15 and having shod your feet with the equipment of the gospel of peace; 16 besides all these, taking the shield of faith, with which you can quench all the flaming darts of the evil one. 17 And take the helmet of salvation, and the sword of the Spirit, which is the word of God. 18 Pray at all times in the Spirit, with all prayer and supplication. To that end keep alert with all perseverance, making supplication for all the saints,*

Why not take a few minutes here and ask the Lord to show you what needs to be brought into the light? Remember, that which is brought into the light cannot have power over you any longer.

⋙━┼━⋘

CHAPTER 12

SOUND THE SHOFAR

The Lord calls us to do many things for Him over the course of a day, a week, a month, a lifetime. Sometimes what He asks might seem a bit ridiculous. He needs an army of believers on the front lines ready to battle for souls, spread His word, and to pray for His people. We must be able to break free from what people might think about us or what they might say about us if we are going to be all in for Jesus! He called me forward one step at a time.

What would you do if one day in prayer the Lord told you to sound the shofar? How would you respond? You see, we are all called to sound the shofar. I want to be a "yes girl" for the Lord, so I literally took the Lord at His word and began to search for a shofar. I was amazed that in a very short time I had a very special one brought to me from the Holy Land. Amazingly, I picked up the skill to blow it pretty quickly.

Many people that I've come in contact with do not know what a shofar is. I actually knew very little about this beautiful instrument myself. So I began to study, research and watch YouTube videos to learn about this awesome instrument. A shofar is an ancient musical instrument made of ram's horn. It is typically used for Jewish religious purposes but anyone can use this special instrument.

The shofar is blown in synagogue services on Rosh Hashanah and at the very end of Yom Kippur, and is also blown every weekday morning in the month of Elul, running up to Rosh Hashanah. Shofars come in a variety of sizes and shapes, depending on the choice of animal and level of finish.

The more I studied about the shofar, the more interested I got. I discerned that the Lord meant for me to literally sound the shofar. If the Lord says to do it, you best obey.

As I prayed and studied about the shofar, I realized that He also wanted me to literally be the shofar. He wanted me to be His mouthpiece. God was actually calling me to do both. The point isn't whether you are being called to blow the shofar. What I think the Lord wants you and me to know is that you are His shofar. You are His instrument that He wants to use to bless His children. He wants your voice to go out and breathe His word into everyone you meet. Ask God to show you the unique way that He wants to use you. Nothing gives me greater enjoyment in life than serving Him and you can have this joy too! Co-laboring with the Lord brings salvation to your soul and to those to whom you minister.

It has been my observation that most of the time, the Lord won't just throw you out into the front lines without preparing you first. All of the stories I've shared have happened over the course of my lifetime and God is still working on me. I don't think that I would have known the full meaning of what God was saying and doing concerning the shofar 40 years ago, but I do now.

It is one thing to pray for people privately in your home (and we should) but it is another to be bold and courageous in the marketplace praying for those the Lord puts into your path. The same goes for giving testimony! Around the same time that the Lord began to call me to be more publicly aware of praying for people in the marketplace is about the same time that he called me out to sound the shofar in public.

Blowing the shofar in your home doesn't take a lot of courage, but it is a whole different experience when you're told to go public! It takes courage to serve the Lord in whatever way He calls you. Do you want to be a warrior? Just ask for the courage and leave the rest up to God.

I was lying in bed one night and I felt an inspiration from the Holy Spirit. I had just finished watching a powerful video on YouTube called "Shofar War Soundtrack." To this day, every time I listen to this video, I cry. It moves me to enter into deep worship and it touches the depths of my soul. After I listened to the soundtrack, I heard the Lord tell me that He wanted me to blow my shofar in church the next day, which happened to be Pentecost Sunday. At this late hour I was sure that my pastor would be hesitant to my request, so I wasn't too concerned about the possibility of doing this at all. I just knew he would say no to my request.

The way that I approached this whole thought process was in my prayer. It's the only way to test the spirits and see if it is truly God calling you to do something. As I prayed I said: "Lord, if you want me to blow that thing, you better give me the go ahead from Fr. John. If he says no, I'll know it was just me talking to myself."

I felt the Lord wanted to awaken the assembly that morning. We were celebrating the birth of the church. He wanted His people to rally and be ready. After praying, I sent a text to Fr. John. He responded very quickly to me. I got a green light. It was then that I got a bit fearful! What on earth had I gotten myself into? I asked him if I could do a couple of minutes of teaching before I just paraded up to the altar area to sound the shofar and he agreed that that would be good.

I'll have to admit that it took some courage to walk into my church carrying the ram's horn, but I felt called to do it and my pastor was behind me. It was Pentecost and I was ready. There were many thoughts running through my head that Sunday. Would people laugh? Would they judge me to be unstable? Would my pastor get complaints and then have to endure hardship because of me? Would I be able to blow it with the proper sound coming out or would it just sound like a cow dying?

The bottom line: I was going to obey God even if I made a fool of myself! I did my teaching and then I sounded that Ram's horn like it was heralding the second coming of Jesus! I felt a victory over fear and a sense of joy and accomplishment when it was all said and done. I had people thank me, but it really didn't matter at that moment if I was judged or not; I was doing what God had asked of me.

The take away lesson was that Jesus was not accepted by all. He suffered ridicule, judgments, and he was even accused of being crazy by his own relatives. ***Mark 3:21 21 When his own family heard that he was there, they went out to seize him, for they said, "He's insane!"***

But that didn't stop Jesus; He went forth obedient to the Father, just as we should. That would not be the last time that I would stand on the wall and sound the horn. The Lord has allowed me to sound the shofar in Washington, D.C., on all four corners of the capital, in New Orleans at a Magnificat Conference, in the Basilica of the Immaculate Conception in Washington, D.C., at San Juan Capistrano, and at many conferences in different states.

I think that being like a shofar is what you would call a fire starter; someone who can cheer the people on to victory in the spirit realm.

What are the lessons that the shofar has taught me and can teach you? Here are some of the things that I have learned and I think that they are lessons we all need to know for the journey.

1. The very shape of the shofar is much like us. It is twisted and unique in shape much like we are. We are sinners twisted and blemished, but when God's breath and life is blown through us, we can bring glory to God. I acknowledge my brokenness and then use that for the glory of God as I share the Gospel and my stories with others.

2. The shofar reminds us of the ram that was provided for Abraham as the sacrifice instead of his own son. We are redeemed through the blood of the lamb, Jesus Christ. He is the perfect sacrifice and atonement for our sins. **Genesis 22:13 - *And Abraham lifted up his eyes and looked, and behold, behind him was a ram, caught in a thicket by his horns; and Abraham went and took the ram, and offered it up as a burnt offering instead of his son.*** I do not have to work myself to death for my salvation and neither do you! Jesus did that for us.

3. The shofar announces that God is King over all. It reminds us that all kingdoms must bow before God almighty. **Psalm 47 - *Clap your hands, all peoples! Shout to God with loud songs of joy! 2 For the Lord, the Most High, is terrible, a great king over all the earth 3 He subdued peoples under us and nations under our feet. 4 He chose our heritage for us, the pride of Jacob whom he loves. Selah 5 God has gone up with a shout, the Lord with the sound of a trumpet. 6 Sing praises to God, sing praises! Sing praises to our King, sing praises! 7 For God is the king of all the earth; sing praises with a psalm! 8 God reigns over the nations; God sits on his holy throne. 9 The princes of the peoples gather as the people of the God of Abraham. For the shields of the earth belong to God; he is highly exalted!*** Is Jesus sitting on the throne of your heart? Is He Lord over it? If not, who or what is a bigger priority in your life?

4. The shofar was used to call the people to worship. *And the four living creatures, each of them with six wings, are full of eyes all round and within, and day and night they never cease to sing, "Holy, holy, holy, is the Lord God Almighty, who was and is and is to come!" 9 And whenever the living creatures give glory and honor and thanks to him who is seated on the throne, who lives for ever and ever, 10 the twenty-four elders fall down before him who is seated on the throne and worship him who*

lives for ever and ever; they cast their crowns before the throne, singing, 11"Worthy art thou, our Lord and God, to receive glory and honor and power, for thou didst create all things, and by thy will they existed and were created." - **Revelation 4: 8-11** We are all called to worship our king! Do we spend time with the Lord each day? Is that time truly spent in praise and worship of God?

5. The shofar is an instrument of warfare. It was used in battle and walls came tumbling down. It confused the enemy camp and brought victory to God's people. What walls need to come down in your life? *And the Lord said to Joshua, "See, I have given into your hand Jericho, with its king and mighty men of valor. 3 You shall march around the city, all the men of war going around the city once. Thus shall you do for six days. 4 And seven priests shall bear seven trumpets of rams' horns before the ark; and on the seventh day you shall march around the city seven times, the priests blowing the trumpets. 5 And when they make a long blast with the ram's horn, as soon as you hear the sound of the trumpet, then all the people shall shout with a great shout; and the wall of the city will fall down flat, and the people shall go up every man straight before him." -* **Joshua 6:2-5** Are you willing to do battle for another? Not in a violent way, but God's way of prayer and fasting?

6. The shofar is used to awaken a slumbering soul. What is inside you that needs to be awakened? Your heart, eyes, tongue, prayer life? *Joel 2: Blow the trumpet in Zion; sound the alarm on my holy mountain! Let all the inhabitants of the land tremble, for the day of the Lord is coming, it is near*

7. It is an instrument of praise. It opens the heavens and brings God's glory. Are we thankful? Do we praise God for all He has done? *As soon as the ark of the covenant of the Lord came into the camp, all Israel gave a mighty shout, so that the earth resounded. -* **1 Samuel 4:5** *They swore an oath to the Lord*

with a loud voice and with shouting and with trumpets and with horns. - **2 Chronicles 15:14** When the ark of the covenant was brought in, the people danced and sang the praises of God. Can you freely worship God in total abandonment?

8. God sounded the shofar on Mount Horeb as He gave the law to Moses. Does God's word make you tremble in awe and respect to his authority? I'm not talking of fear-based respect but obedience because of love. **Exodus 19:16-22 -** *16 On the morning of the third day there were thunders and lightnings, and a thick cloud upon the mountain, and a very loud trumpet blast, so that all the people who were in the camp trembled. 17 Then Moses brought the people out of the camp to meet God; and they took their stand at the foot of the mountain. 18 And Mount Sinai was wrapped in smoke, because the Lord descended upon it in fire; and the smoke of it went up like the smoke of a kiln, and the whole mountain quaked greatly. 19 And as the sound of the trumpet grew louder and louder, Moses spoke, and God answered him in thunder. 20 And the Lord came down upon Mount Sinai, to the top of the mountain; and the Lord called Moses to the top of the mountain, and Moses went up. 21 And the Lord said to Moses, "Go down and warn the people, lest they break through to the Lord to gaze and many of them perish. 22 And also let the priests who come near to the Lord consecrate themselves, lest the Lord break out upon them."*

9. The shofar calls us to repentance and to fasting, It was used at specific times to remind the people to step back and examine the past year in relation to their actions to God and others. We have to listen to God just like the sound of the shofar and hear internally where God wants us to repent and heal us. I must reflect and make a good examination of conscience and then avail myself of the sacrament of reconciliation. **Ephesians 5:13-14 -** *13 but when anything is exposed by the light it becomes visible, for anything that becomes*

*visible is light. 14 Therefore it is said, "Awake, O sleeper, and
arise from the dead, and Christ shall give you light."*

10. The shofar reminds us that on the last day, God will sound
the shofar at His second coming. Am I prepared? Are you?
**Matthew 24:31 - *31 and he will send out his angels with a loud
trumpet call, and they will gather his elect from the four winds,
from one end of heaven to the other.***

Yes, we are called to be the shofar. How we sound that shofar is
discerned through prayer and direction. St. Ignatius teaches us to
be very discerning. As I mentioned before, not all good things are
good for us. We must pray and discern what it is that God wants from
us. It was probably 20 years ago that I went to a Magnificat meal in
northern Arkansas. Magnificat is a ministry for Catholic women,
although women of other faiths are surely welcome! Magnificat's
mission is to evangelize and to encourage Catholic women to grow
in holiness through opening more fully to the power and the gifts
of the Holy Spirit.

Magnificat's objectives are to: 1.) live out the mystery of Mary's
visit to Elizabeth 2.) help Catholic women to open more and more
to the Holy Spirit through a deeper commitment of their lives to
Jesus as Lord and to impart the Holy Spirit to one another by their
love, service, and sharing the good news of salvation, 3.) provide
opportunities which foster growth in holiness, 4.) sponsor the
Magnificat Meal, the essential function of Magnificat, and 5.) imi-
tate Mary through spiritual adoption of priests and seminarians.

It was the chapter's first official function. I was much younger
with small children in my home. As I absorbed all that the day had
to give, I left there with a desire to bring something like this to
central Arkansas. I remember going home and reading about this
ministry on the internet. That desire was a seed planted that had
to lay dormant in the soil of my soul for a long time. It was a great
ministry but it just wasn't right for me and my family at that time.

What I did discern was that my home parish could have something for the women in our parish. It was doable for my position in life, and by the direction of the Holy Spirit with a very dedicated core team of women, we birthed what we call "Woman to Woman." It is a retreat weekend that has been going on in our parish now for some 15 years.

As I was called into the Woman to Woman Ministry, I was also called out. Ministry is like that. It can be like the waves of the ocean. An ebb and flow. You have to be able to read the waves and go with them or they will knock you down. I just had a knowing that it was time to step back. When we listen and do just that, God brings in new leadership and that is always good. Someone else will learn how to sound the shofar.

I was at Mass one weekday morning when the Lord started knocking on my heart once again. I clearly heard Him say interiorly, it's time to start Magnificat in Central Arkansas. I hadn't thought about the desire to bring Magnificat to Central Arkansas in many years. Actually it was 10 years later and the seed was beginning to awaken in the soil of my soul. I knew it was a true call so what did I do? I went home and called the central office for Magnificat in New Orleans and the process began.

There are many checks and balances that someone must go through to start a chapter and they are there for a reason. If the call hadn't been from the Lord, our core team of five would have thrown in the towel. We are now in our fifth year as a chapter and it is amazing to see how this ministry touches the lives of so many women. Each woman who attends is being blessed, healed, and learning how to be a shofar for the Lord. This is one time that it's a good thing to toot your own horn! There's a sisterhood with the women and I've made friends with women from all over the world! I'm proud to be a part of an International Ministry that renews and touches the lives of so many women.

You've heard about my call to become a Spiritual Director. This ministry brings me great joy. I feel so privileged and humbled to be able to walk alongside someone's interior life. As I walk with them, I learn more about myself. Unlike other ministries I've been involved with, it is very contemplative and we all need to develop a contemplative approach to life.

Embracing my own broken places has helped me to sit with others in theirs. I've learned that the kingdom of heaven starts here and now. Spiritual Direction has taught me to slow down and savor life. To be present to God in the now moments. Somehow, as I've slowed down, quit talking so much and started to listen more, I've regained that sense of freedom that I learned on the farm so many years ago. To quote my daughter Tara: "It's not only about the destination, but the journey that it takes to get there."

As I have reflected on my life while writing this book, it has become clear that God has worked with me day in and day out. Your life and mine are like paintings on a canvas. The beauty of the finished work is brought about one stroke at a time. It's not until the last stroke is placed on the canvas that the artist wants to frame their work for others to admire. When people see the finished painting it moves and inspires them to appreciate all that the painting represents.

All of life is preparation for our final glory. My heart's desire is that no one who comes in contact with me misses an opportunity to see Jesus lived out in my words and actions because I didn't do my part. I don't know about you, but I'm going to be blowing the shofar one step at a time. I want to look at Jesus eye-to-eye when I get to heaven and hear Him say: ***"Well done, good and faithful servant; you have been faithful over a little, I will set you over much; enter into the joy of your master."*** **- Matthew 25:23.**

Don't you want this too? Holding the healing hand of God is exciting and rewarding! I leave you with one last question: "What is God calling you to do and how will you answer His call?" Sound the shofar! Let the walls tumble down! You and God are an overwhelming majority.

St. Teresa of the Child Jesus is my patron saint. I have a plaque on my living room wall that has inspired me for many years. The plaque has a quote from St. Teresa on it and the first time I read it, the words burned in my heart deeply. It still inspires me to this day. It says:

> I want to love you like a little child.
> I want to fight like a brave warrior.
> Like a child full of little attentions, Lord, I want to overwhelm
> you with caresses, and in the field of the apostolate,
> like a warrior I throw myself into the fight!
> Your heart that preserves innocence, won't betray my trust!
> In you Lord rests my hope.
> When in my heart the storm arises, to you Jesus,
> I lift up my head.
> In your merciful look I read: Child for you I made the heavens."

ADDENDUM

As the pages of this book were written, I followed the lead of the Holy Spirit. There are, however, a few suggestions that I would like to add to this book. As you read each chapter see if the Holy Spirit is nudging you in some way. Ask the Lord questions as you come across something that may stretch you a bit. It is my opinion that when we get a bit antsy and defensive the Lord may be trying to breakthrough in some way. Don't rush over the concept. Just talk to the Lord and then listen in prayer. A particular concept or grace that you are praying through might take a long time to discern; weeks, months, or sometimes years. Do the work, you'll be glad you did.

If you are a new believer, use all kinds of resources to get you in the habit of daily prayer. Catholics have many great resources from which to choose. The Word Among Us, Magnificat, Living Faith, Our Daily Bread, Jesus Calling, and the *Liturgy of the Hours* are just a few printed materials. If you are into using your smart phone you can use the Laudate App with daily Mass readings, The Examen app is great to help you look back on your awareness of God's presence with you each day, and there's daily emails from a plethora of Christian groups. The most important thing is that you get in a daily habit of scripture reading and dialoging with the Lord. The key is not so much to have knowledge of God (which is good) but getting to know who God is through these daily readings and then forming a relationship with him. Daily reading and quiet time with the Lord is how that relationship with Him will be formed. It will take discipline and grace to be still and listen. Don't give up! This will be the start to a joy-filled life no matter what may come. When the going gets tough, you have your friend Jesus to walk with you. When there is great joy, you can share it with your friend Jesus.

Maybe you've been walking with the Lord for a long time but you feel dry or stagnant in your relationship. You've lost the wonder. If that's the case, try switching things up. It could just be that the Lord is trying to get you to try something new because you're just going through the checklist of daily prayer. Think on this example. Have you been in a restaurant and watched couples eating together? Maybe they've been married for a long while but they're not really even talking to each other. Yes, they're there together but because they've become so accustomed to each other and doing the same old thing, they've just lost their way when in each other's company. They may be in the same space physically but they're actually not communicating. Perhaps they need to make a conscious effort to make some changes. This could be how it is between you and the Lord. If it is, don't quit!

Another great help no matter what stage you're in is to take part in the life of your church community. Make friends in like-minded groups that meet regularly such as scripture study groups, charismatic prayer groups, Marian groups, pro-life groups, men's groups, or women's groups. If there is a Magnificat Ministry near you, seek it out and attend when there are functions. There are programs for those who have been away from the church such as Catholics Returning Home. In most every church there is a great need to serve on RCIA teams (rite of Christian initiation of adults), or PRE teachers (Sunday school). These programs will grow you as you help others. Pray and ask the Lord where He wants you. Be careful though to not become just a doer.... you have to just BE with the Lord first to know where and what to do. God has a unique plan for each of us.

There are all kinds of retreat programs as well. For me, the Cursillo movement was a wonderful way to grow with my husband. It is simple, but profound, and was just what we needed in our thirties. The three-day retreat is only part of the process. The real gift is staying strong in what is called the fourth day by meeting weekly with a small group and then monthly with other small groups. This program is also available in other denominations. Some other names of the same program are Walk to Emmaus and Tres Dias. To get more information check with your local diocesan offices or your local church.

If you have a troubled Marriage there is Retrovie. Want to strengthen your marriage, how about Marriage Encounter? Have you had an abortion? Project Rachael is for you. My local parish has parish retreats for men and women yearly. Beside these types of retreats, you may now have interest in a Silent Retreat. Believe me, this type of retreat didn't always appeal to me but now I can't live without that solitude. Some are directed, which means that you meet with a spiritual director for about 45 minutes each day and then pray over the scriptures or directives they give you in the next 24-hour period. These can be from three days to as much as thirty days.

Let me say here that it's not likely that you'll go from a little prayer each day and then jump into a thirty-day retreat. Our faith life is something we build on day after day over the course of our lifetime. Another type of silent retreat is what is called a preached retreat. This is when the group comes together in silence to hear a talk on a particular subject and then leaves for quiet prayer and meditation. The key to all these retreats is to help you to grow your relationship with the Lord and to grow your holiness to be more like Christ. Some helpful links for a silent retreat: jesuits.org, igantianspirituality.com, stmarybythesea.org

As a trained Spiritual Director, I can't express the importance of seeking out a spiritual director. Meeting with someone who can walk with you on your spiritual life is invaluable. Be prepared to grow if you give yourself the gift of Spiritual Direction. It's a slow work, but I promise you that you will grow. Within the dynamics of the Ignatian way of praying, there is a program called Retreat In Daily Life. This is a thirty-week prayer experience developed for those who cannot make a thirty-day silent retreat.

I believe it is of extreme importance to associate with people who have strong faith lives, who will build you up as you walk in the kingdom here and now. If people that you're around right now aren't living for the Lord and are critical of others who are, make some changes in your friendships.

AS I SHARED WITH YOU some of my experiences you may have heard some ideas or words that you were unfamiliar with such as: Charismatic Renewal, disordered desires, lived experience, false self or ego, interior voice, detachment, and interior freedom. Let me give you some brief explanations of these words.

The Charismatic Renewal was life-giving for me. For those of you who are unfamiliar with it in the context of the Catholic Church I would like to offer you some excerpts taken from the United States Conference of Catholic Bishops National Service Committee Charismatic Renewal website on Baptism in the Holy Spirit. "As experienced in the Catholic Charismatic Renewal, baptism in the Holy Spirit makes Jesus Christ known and loved as Lord and Savior, establishes or reestablishes an immediacy of relationship with all those persons on the Trinity, and through inner transformation affects the whole of the Christian's life. There is new life and a new conscious awareness of God's power and presence. It is a grace experience which touches every dimension of the Church's life: worship, preaching, teaching, ministry, evangelism, prayer and spirituality, service and community. Because of this, it is our conviction that baptism in the Holy Spirit, understood as the reawakening in Christian experience of the presence and action of the Holy Spirit given in Christian initiation, and manifested in a broad range of charisms, including those closely associated with the Catholic Charismatic Renewal, is part of the normal Christian life."

Pope Paul VI and Pope John Paul II both made enthusiastic statements in favor of the renewal. For more information about the renewal visit: https://www.nsc-chariscenter.org

DESIRE IS SOMETHING that we all have. It is a common experience to desire certain things or feelings. When we desire something we must decide if it will bring life to us or if it will be a quick fix or patch to some deeper desire that we really are seeking – such as the desire to love. Do we seek the pure form of love that is life-giving or do we seek a quick fix that satisfies us temporarily but only leaves us emptier after acting upon the disordered desire. Another way to look at it would be that a disordered desire is allowing the desire to control us instead of us controlling the desire in a healthy way. Disordered desires enslave us and will lead us into sin and away from God.

LIVED EXPERIENCES are just that. They are situations that we have lived through and from which we have gained some type of knowledge or experience. For instance, it's easy to talk about how a person should respond to a pregnancy out of wedlock, but until you've lived that experience, your ideas are mere concepts and not from actual life experience. If you've lost a child, you've lived that experience. It will be so much more life-giving for you to speak to someone who is in that situation than someone who means well in what they say, but has never experienced what they're talking about.

INTERIOR VOICE is the thoughts or feelings we get in our head or gut. The most important thing about an interior voice is discerning if it is the voice of God, or our own thoughts, or the dark one coming cloaked as an angel of light. A good place to get great information about this is from a website: ignatiansprituality. com.

INTERIOR FREEDOM is when we can become detached from things, ideas or circumstances in such a way that no matter what comes our way nothing can disturb our inner peace because we have complete faith, hope, and trust in God alone. We know that God is the source of our peace and freedom, and He alone is our sure guarantee for that type of freedom. The following is taken from the book *Interior Freedom.*

"True freedom is not so much something man wins for himself; it is a free gift from God, a fruit of the Holy Spirit, received in the measure in which we place ourselves in a relationship of loving dependence on our Creator and Savior. This is where the Gospel paradox is most apparent: 'Whoever would save his life will lose it, and whoever loses his life for my sake will find it.' In other words, people who wish to preserve and defend their own freedom at any cost will lose it, but those willing to 'lose' it by leaving it trustingly in God's hands will save it. Their freedom will be restored to them, infinitely more beautiful, infinitely deeper, as a marvelous gift from God's tenderness. Our freedom is, in fact, proportionate to the love and childlike trust we have for our heavenly Father."

- Interior Freedom, p.14-15, Jacques Philippe

The following excerpt on DETACHMENT is from the book *In the School of the Holy Spirit:*

"To allow ourselves to be led by the Spirit of God, we need great compliance and adaptability, and we can acquire these little by little by practicing detachment. We should make an effort not to "hang on to" anything, either materially, or affectively, or even spiritually. The detachment we should aim for is not that of saying "to hell with all of it," or of becoming indifferent to everything, or of practicing a sort of forced asceticism and stripping ourselves of everything that makes up our lives; that kind of detachment is not what our Lord normally asks for. But we need to keep our hearts in an attitude of detachment, maintaining a sort of freedom, a distance, an inner reserve, that will mean that if some particular thing, or habit, or relationship, or personal plan is taken from us, we don't make a drama out of being deprived of it. Such detachment should be exercised in all aspects of our lives."

- In the School of the Holy Spirit, p.35 Jacques Philippe

I've chosen an excerpt from Richard Rohr to explain your FALSE SELF. He certainly can explain it far better than I can. I think this is such an important concept and I believe understanding this helps you to live in greater freedom.

"Your egoic false self is who you think you are, but your thinking does not make it true. Your false self is a social and mental construct to get you started on your life journey. It is a set of agreements between you and your parents, your family, your school chums, your partner or spouse, your culture, and your religion. It is your "container." It is largely defined in distinction from others, precisely as your separate and unique self. It is probably necessary to get started, but it becomes problematic when you stop there and spend the rest of your life promoting and protecting it.

"Jesus would call your false self your "wineskin," which he points out is only helpful insofar as it can contain some good and new wine. He says that "old wineskins" cannot hold any new wine; in fact, "they burst and both the skins and the wine are lost" (Luke 5:37-38). This is a quite telling and wise metaphor, revealing Jesus' bias toward growth and change. "The old wine is good enough" (Luke 5:39), says the man or woman set in their ways.

"The false self, which we might also call the "small self," is merely your launching pad: your appearance, your education, your job, your money, your success, and so on. These are the trappings of ego that help you get through an ordinary day. They are what Bill Plotkin wisely calls your "survival dance," but they are not yet your "sacred dance." [1]

"Please understand that your false self is not bad or inherently deceitful. Your false self is actually quite good and necessary as far as it goes. It just does not go far enough, and it often poses and thus substitutes for the real thing. That is its only problem, and that is why we call it "false." The false self is bogus more than bad; it pretends to be more than it is. Various false selves (temporary costumes) are necessary to get us all started, but they show their limitations when they stay around too long. If people keep growing, their various false selves usually die in exposure to greater light. That is, if they ever let greater light get in; many do not.

"When you are able to move beyond your false self—at the right time and in the right way—it will feel as if you have lost nothing. Of course, if all you know is the false self and you do not know that there is anything "beyond" it, the transition will probably feel like dying. Only after you have fallen into the True Self, will you be able to say with the mystic Rumi, "What have I ever lost by dying?" [2] You have discovered true freedom and liberation. When you are connected to the Whole, you no longer need to protect or defend the part. You are now connected to something inexhaustible.

"If you do not let go of your false self at the right time and in the right way, you remain stuck, trapped, and addicted. (The traditional word for that was sin.) Unfortunately, many people reach old age still entrenched in their egoic operating system. Only your True Self lives forever and is truly free in this world."

References:

[1] Bill Plotkin, Soulcraft: Crossing into the Mysteries of Nature and Psyche (New World Library: 2003), 84.

[2] Rumi, "Tell Me, What Have I Lost?" in The Winged Energy of Delight: Selected Translations, trans. Robert Bly (Harper Perennial: 2005), 339.

Adapted from Richard Rohr, Immortal Diamond: The Search for Our True Self (Jossey-Bass: 2013), 27-29, 36.

I pray this book has blessed you and that it has caused you to want more of the Blessed Trinity. Thank you for allowing me to share some of myself, but a whole lot more about our awesome God!

- Debbie Eckert
July 2018

ACKNOWLEDGEMENTS

I would first and foremost like to give thanks to our awesome God! It is by His grace that each word in this book was written. It was a surprise to me when He called these pages forth; however, I've always had a love for writing and sharing my faith with others. Responding to His call with the best of my ability has been a joy and a challenge. As the saying goes "No pain, no gain."

To my mom and dad who have gone before me, thank you for passing my Catholic faith to me. Special thanks goes to my father in law Ken Eckert for his love and generosity.

To my loving, precious husband, my love and thanks goes to you from the bottom of my heart. Kenny, you have lived with this "work in progress" for some time now, and I have so loved your support and words of wisdom. You were good to keep me on even keel and you always have been my biggest fan and encourager. As each day passes, I know more of how much God loves me because of the love and sacrifices that you have given me. It's been a great ride doing life with you. I love you forever!

Trey, Laura, Tara, Jason, Anthony, Meridee, Abbey and Ben, my eyes fill with tears of gratitude as I think of the love you each have given me. For the numerous calls and texts, and drafts and constant listening that you had to endure, I am grateful. Each time that you gave your love and support blessed me and encouraged me to keep on writing. It is my desire that I have left you and your precious children, and those that are still yet to be, a legacy of word and actions.

To you my precious grandchildren, Parker, Alec, Delaney, Macy, Channing, Maddie, Saylor, Rory, Benjamin and those that are yet to come, Maw Maw loves you "deerly." Keep the faith and serve the Lord with all your heart .

Special thanks to Helen Plotkin, my editor, for the first words you spoke that gave me courage to believe in myself and all your hard work editing. Sandra Ake artist, extraordinaire, you will never know how much your gift has blessed me. Kitty Cleveland, thank you for calling my gift forward. These pages might not have ever been written if not for the Lord using you to speak it into being. To my very special girlfriends who have believed in me and encouraged me in so many ways, I love you and your honesty. For those who have taken time to review this book... Gracias.

Finally, to my beloved priests whom I intercede for daily, thank you for all your prayers and sacrifices and encouragement. A special thanks to my "brother" John Marconi.

- Debbie Eckert
July 2018

ABOUT THE AUTHOR

Debbie Eckert is passionate, driven, and all in for the Lord. Debbie is married to her spouse of forty-five years Ken, and they have four married children with nine grandchildren whose ages range from 22 to one year old. Being a wife and mother is her first and most important apostolate.

Debbie, a hairstylist for 48 years, has owned her own business for 38 of those years. In addition to her commitment to her family and business, Debbie has been an evangelist for the Lord within the Diocese of Arkansas. She served as the Executive Director for the Cursillo Ministry in her diocese for six years, founded the Jesus Bread of Life Magnificat chapter in Central Arkansas, and has been the Coordinator for that ministry since its beginning.

She completed four years of training through her diocese to become an Ignatian Spiritual Director. She has spoken at various conferences, Magnificat meals, and Life in the Spirit seminars, and has served in just about every capacity in her parish. As a directive from the Holy Spirit, Debbie founded the Woman to Woman retreat program for St. Joseph's parish. She has been involved in the Charismatic renewal for more than 38 years.

Her salon, known as "Debbie's Hair and Prayer," is where she ministers daily behind her styling chair.

Made in the USA
Columbia, SC
23 July 2019